PENGUIN MODERN CLASSIC

C000235862

Collected Poems

Vladimir Nabokov (1899–1977) was one of the great writers of the twentieth century, as well as a translator and lepidopterist. His works include *The Luzhin Defense*, *The Gift*, *Lolita*, *Pnin*, *Pale Fire* and *Ada or Ardor*; the autobiographical *Speak, Memory*; and lectures on literature. All of the fiction and *Speak, Memory* are published in Penguin.

Dmitri Nabokov (1934–2012) was one of Vladimir Nabokov's principal translators, from and into four languages. After graduating with honours from Harvard and attending the Longy School of Music, he performed leading bass roles in opera houses in a number of countries.

VLADIMIR NABOKOV

Collected Poems

Edited and Introduced by Thomas Karshan
Containing New Translations by Dmitri Nabokov

PENGUIN BOOKS

PENGUIN CLASSICS

Published by the Penguin Group
Penguin Books Ltd, 80 Strand, London WC2R ORL, England
Penguin Group (USA) Inc., 375 Hudson Street, New York, New York 10014, USA
Penguin Group (Canada), 90 Eglinton Avenue East, Suite 700, Toronto, Ontario,
Canada M4P 2Y3 (a division of Pearson Penguin Canada Inc.)
Penguin Ireland, 25 St Stephen's Green, Dublin 2, Ireland (a division of Penguin Books Ltd)
Penguin Group (Australia), 707 Collins Street, Melbourne, Victoria 3008, Australia
(a division of Pearson Australia Group Pty Ltd)
Penguin Books India Pvt Ltd, 11 Community Centre, Panchsheel Park,
New Delhi – 110 017, India
Penguin Group (NZ), 67 Apollo Drive, Rosedale, Auckland 0632, New Zealand
(a division of Pearson New Zealand Ltd)
Penguin Books (South Africa) (Pty) Ltd, Block D, Rosebank Office Park,
181 Jan Smuts Avenue, Parktown North, Gauteng 2193, South Africa

Penguin Books Ltd, Registered Offices: 80 Strand, London WC2R ORL, England

www.penguin.com

First published by Penguin Classics 2012
This paperback edition published 2013
003

Copyright © Vladimir Nabokov, 1920, 1923, 1941, 1942, 1943, 1944, 1945, 1946,
1950, 1951, 1952, 1953, 1955, 1956, 1957, 1966, 1970, 1991
Translations copyright © Dmitri Nabokov, 1984, 1988, 1989, 1990, 1992,
1998, 1999, 2000, 2003, 2005, 2008, 2012
Introduction and editorial material copyright © Thomas Karshan, 2012

Printed in Great Britain by Clays Ltd, St Ives plc

ISBN: 978-0-141-19226-0

www.greenpenguin.co.uk

Contents

The Russian Poems from
Poems and Problems

The English Poems from
Poems and Problems

English Poems Not Included in
Poems and Problems

Introduction

Like Joyce, Nabokov was first a poet. It was, he tells us in his autobiography *Speak, Memory* (1967), 'the summer of 1914 ... when the numb fury of verse-making first came over me'.[1] Over the next decade he composed thousands of poems, which he came, years later, to remember with a certain fond disgust: in the introduction to his 1970 collection *Poems and Problems*, he would speak of 'the steady mass of verse which I began to exude in my early youth, more than half a century ago ... with monstrous regularity'.[2] Many, if not most, of these early poems were never published, though some did appear in his first collection, *Stikhi* (*Poems*), published in 1916 while the Nabokov family was still in Russia, and a few more in 1918, in a collection which also included the poems of a school-friend, Andrei Balashov. After the Revolution, and the Nabokov family's emigration to Western Europe in 1919, Nabokov continued to write poetry, first as an undergraduate at Cambridge from 1919 to 1922, and then in Berlin, where he rejoined his family and entered the thriving literary culture of the Russian emigration. There he found public outlets for his verse in the Russian-language press, especially the Berlin émigré newspaper *Rul'* (the *Rudder*), of which Nabokov's father was a founder-editor; in turn, thirty-six of his poems were collected into a volume entitled *The Cluster* in December 1922, and another 156 in *The Empyrean Path* in January 1923.

After 1926, when Nabokov published his first novel *Mary*, he wrote markedly fewer poems, and his lyric impulse was largely channelled into his novels: after all, Nabokov ranks alongside James Joyce, Marcel Proust, and Samuel Beckett as one of those great modernists who reinvented the novel as a vehicle for poetic prose. Indeed, his last and most important

Russian novel, *The Gift* (published serially in 1937–8 and in its complete form in 1952), a fictionalized semi-autobiography, is the story of a young poet, Fyodor, successfully turning himself into a novelist. Nevertheless, the poems which Nabokov did write after 1926 make up in interest and individuality for their scarcity in comparison with his earlier output. They also complement the fiction, addressing many of the same ideas and themes; indeed many of these newer poems appeared alongside Nabokov's stories in the 1929 collection *The Return of Chorb*.

After *Chorb*, Nabokov did not produce another collection of verse until the 1950s, when two slim volumes appeared: in 1952, *Stikhotvoreniia 1929–1951* (*Poems 1929–1951*), which contains fifteen Russian poems, including a group of significant long poems he wrote in the late 1930s and early 1940s; and, in 1959, *Poems*, made up of fourteen of the poems Nabokov had written in English after going to America in 1940, most of which had first appeared in the *New Yorker* magazine. These fourteen poems were in turn republished in *Poems and Problems* in 1970, alongside thirty-nine of the Russian poems which Nabokov translated for the volume. Finally, in 1979 – two years after his death – was published another selection of the Russian poems, entitled, simply, *Stikhi*, or *Poems*. In addition to the major Russian poems of the period between 1925 and 1945, this volume also contained some of the earlier verse, including some previously unpublished poems.

Since the late 1980s, Nabokov's son, Dmitri – a distinguished translator who worked with his father on turning many of the novels into English – has been publishing translations of Nabokov's poems in various journals. In the present volume, these translations (sometimes revised) are reprinted alongside translations that have never before appeared – including Dmitri Nabokov's translation of the novella-length *The University Poem* (1927),[3] which will make a significant addition to the corpus of his father's work available in Russian, and 'Music', a poem from that poetry-writing summer of 1914, whose Russian original has never been printed, and which is therefore the earliest work by Nabokov now available. Also included are the nine poems written in English which Nabokov did not include in *Poems and Problems* – these being the three early poems from 1920 to 1923, four poems from the 1940s, and a couple of slighter but still interesting pieces of verse.

Four aspects of this edition should be noted. First, and regrettably, it has not been possible to include two components of *Poems and Problems* – the chess problems which Nabokov appended to the verse, and the original Russian text of the poems he placed beside his translations. Second, the decision was made not to print the poems chronologically but to present them in three separate sections: Dmitri Nabokov's new translations; then all the poems, Russian translations and English originals, from *Poems and Problems*; then the nine English poems which did not appear in *Poems and Problems*. The cost of this choice is that the volume does not present the poems in a single unbroken chronological sequence, but the benefits are that it maintains a clear distinction between Nabokov's own writing and the translations by his son, and that it preserves the integrity of *Poems and Problems*. The poems from *Poems and Problems* appear in exactly the same sequence as in the original publication, even though this sequence does not always reflect what we now know to be the chronology of composition and publication; it was felt inappropriate to rearrange a volume Nabokov had personally overseen. The other poems in this volume are presented, within each section, in chronological sequence according to date of composition, where that is known, and otherwise by date of publication. Third, the spelling of the poems from *Poems and Problems* – almost entirely American rather than British in style – has been preserved; and all other poems in the volume have been regularized to conform with this for the sake of consistency.

Lastly, it should be noted that John Shade's poem 'Pale Fire', a major part of the 1962 novel of the same name, is not included in this present volume. Nor are the many other poems scattered through Nabokov's work, and attributed to various characters in them – such as Fyodor's poems in *The Gift*, or Humbert Humbert's in *Lolita* (1955). Whatever their merits, these poems are all meant to characterize their fictional authors: Fyodor, Shade, Humbert. Admittedly, the distinction between poems written by Nabokov, and those written by individuals Nabokov invented, may be a shaky one; even in the verse printed in this volume, Nabokov adopts many different personae, and in a few cases, such as 'The Paris Poem' (1943) and 'L'Inconnue de la Seine' (1934), the poems even originally appeared under a pseudonym – in the latter instance, that of Fyodor. Still, however Nabokovian such subtleties about authorship may be, the choice of poems excluded from this volume has been dictated by brutal common sense: those not ultimately signed as Nabokov's 'own' are not here, and not least because they can be obtained elsewhere, and in their proper context.

In the introduction to *Poems and Problems*, Nabokov offered a summing-up of his poetic career that demands to be quoted here in full:

> What can be called rather grandly my European period of verse-making seems to show several distinctive stages: an initial one of passionate and commonplace love verse ... a period reflecting utter distrust of the so-called October Revolution; a period (reaching well into the 1920s) of a kind of private curatorship, aimed at preserving nostalgic retrospections and developing Byzantine imagery (this has been mistaken by some readers for an interest in 'religion', which, beyond literary stylization, never meant anything to me); a period lasting another decade or so during which I set myself to illustrate the principle of making a short poem contain a plot and tell a story (this in a way expressed my impatience with the dreary drone of the anemic 'Paris School' of *émigré* poetry); and finally, in the late thirties, and especially in the following decades, a sudden liberation from self-imposed shackles, resulting both in a sparser output and in a belatedly discovered robust style ...
>
> There is not much to say about the section of fourteen English poems, all written in America and all published in *The New Yorker*. Somehow, they are of a lighter texture than the Russian stuff, owing, no doubt, to their lacking that inner verbal association with old perplexities and constant worry of thought which marks poems written in one's mother tongue, with exile keeping up its parallel murmur and a never-resolved childhood plucking at one's rustiest chords.[4]

As Nabokov briskly outlines here, his poetry, over the course of the fifty-nine years spanned by the poems in this volume, passed through many changes of style and subject. Yet there is a quality his poems nearly all possess, which is likely to be the first thing that will strike a reader coming to them from a familiarity with Nabokov's extraordinarily sophisticated novels: a bold simplicity, appearing, at times, to border even on naïveté. In late middle age, the by-then famous author of *Lolita* wasted few opportunities to inform interviewers that 'art is never simple': 'To return to my lecturing days: I automatically gave low marks when a student used the dreadful phrase "simple and sincere".'[5] Yet anyone surveying Nabokov's poems from a list of their opening lines will find displayed there a lyric landscape which, for over fifty years, remained one of ardent declarations, ingenuous exclamations, and straightforward narratives: 'I dream of simple tender things' (1923); 'I like that mountain in its black pelisse' (1925); 'For happiness the lover cannot sleep' (1928); 'Oh, that sound! Across snow – / creak, creak, creak' (1930); 'What happened overnight to memory?' (1938); 'Will you leave me alone? I implore you!' (1939); 'When he was small, when he would fall' (1942); 'That Sunday morning, at half past ten, / Two cars crossed the creek and entered the glen' (1957); 'Forty-three years, forty-four years maybe' (1967).

The poems often take place on the same familiar dusty stage-set, inherited from Romanticism: a man sits alone in a moonlit room, looking out of an open window, assailed by the unresolved memories of a lost and unrecoverable past. The conceit behind each poem tends to be easy to grasp, its execution pursued without any of the twists and turns of Nabokov's novelistic intelligence. The stanzaic forms of the poems are also usually traditional – frequently quatrains rhyming *abab* – as are the rhythms, which are often, though not always, insistently iambic.[6] And many if not most of the poems are formed on the rhetorical device of apostrophe, in which the poet speaks directly not only to people and objects, but even to abstract entities. Among Nabokov's addressees are: the Muse; the poet; angels; his younger self; his heart; his soul; his precious being; his inevitable day; Russia; Liberty; Recollection; Joan of Arc; an imaginary Prince Kachurin; Shakespeare; his dead father; a grapefruit.

This frequent recourse to apostrophe in Nabokov's poetry has drawn against it accusations of sentimentality from its earliest reviewers up to the present. But as David Rampton observes in his essay on the subject, 'apostrophe is always sentimental because it conjures up a world in which nature is animate, whether in the form of talking dryads, articulate West Winds, responsive inkwells, or whatever. They are all the plausible inhabitants of a world that can be talked to.'[7] It would be wrong to take all this as empty rhetorical convention. Nabokov may not have really thought the grapefruit he addressed was alive, but his capacity for experiencing every detail of the world as if it were potentially responsive is one of the secrets of his extraordinary imagination, and it corresponds to his idea of the artist as not just a magician but even a shaman – as he put it in 'Fame' (1942): 'To myself I appear as an idol, a wizard / bird-headed, emerald gloved, dressed in tights / made of bright-blue scales.' On this reckoning, it is the gift of the poet to instil the simplest speech-act – a mere greeting, even – with the power to conjure back the dead, to give objects life, and to imbue ideas and words with independence and vitality. Nabokov's most famous sentences, the opening of *Lolita*, are an address ('Lolita, light of my life, fire of my loins'), as are its closing words ('And this is the only immortality you and I may share, my Lolita').[8]

By contrast, in a group of important poems from the late 1930s and early 1940s dealing with his shattering transition from the Russian to the English language, Nabokov explores the basic words and gestures for farewell, and plays painfully on their inadequacy to the tasks he wishes they could perform for him: renunciation, mourning, exorcism. In 'Softest of Tongues' (1941), he whimsically collates the various objects to which he had bid '*prash-chaï*', or 'good-bye' (flats, sky-writing, waiters, cuts, love), and the various ways of bidding farewell ('And so that's that, / you say under your breath, and wave your hand, / and then your handkerchief, and then your hat'), before trying and failing to dismiss Russian itself ('But now too thou must go'). In 'An Evening of Russian Poetry' (1945), Nabokov ends, devastatingly, by allowing the ghosts of his imperfectly exorcised language to speak their reproof, exposing the incapacity of even the simplest English phrase to work its required magic on his psyche: the '*good night*' he is wished becomes, translated through the language of betrayal, an 'insomnia' of 'apostasy'.

Nabokov pledged himself young to the cause of simplicity. Not only 'The Russian Song' (1923) but many of the other early Russian poems express his love of 'simple tender things'. In one such still untranslated poem, also from 1923, the poet stops in at a little shop in Castile to find a magician presiding over the treasury of his extraordinary wares, but leaves the shop to look for 'a single simple word for human love'.[9] This commitment to simplicity was essential to Nabokov's sense of what poetry should be. In the 1920s he put himself firmly in the camp of those conservative modern poets who rejected the free verse, chaotic forms, and perilous leaps of sense of revolutionary poets such as Vladimir Mayakovsky, Boris Pasternak, and Ezra Pound. Thus, in Russian the poets he admired were Nikolai Gumilev, Ivan Bunin, and Vladislav Khodasevich, who harked back to the tradition of Alexander Pushkin and Fyodor Tyutchev (both of whom Nabokov later translated). In English, it was the Georgian poets whom he admitted as influences, especially Walter de la Mare and Rupert Brooke. It was their 'verse patterns', he tells us in *Speak, Memory*, that were 'running about my room and all over me like tame mice',[10] while he devoted himself to becoming a Russian poet as an undergraduate at Cambridge.

In Nabokov's reviews of the 1920s we can already find traces of his mature view of poetry as 'the mysteries of the irrational as perceived through rational words'.[11] His key words of praise are 'clear' or 'intelligible' ('*poniatnyi*' and '*otchëtlivyi*'), 'pure' ('*chistyi*'), 'harmonious' or 'well structured' ('*stroinyi*'), 'correct' ('*pravilnyi*') – and, perhaps most often, 'simple' ('*prostyi*'). In the opening of his first-ever review, published in *Rul'* on 17 December 1922, Nabokov passionately expresses the sentiment that informs all his criticism: 'In our black days, when countless hooligan "poetasters" torture the Russian muse, it is sweet to open a booklet of simple and intelligible verses.' It is no objection to the poet in question that in him Nabokov finds 'the shadow of a somehow pleasing old-fashionedness'.[12] In a review written nearly five years later, on 31 August 1927, Nabokov praises another minor figure, whose 'quiet modest poetry is, as it were, written not in emigration, but in a thicket of alder-trees, in a miraculously unchanged leafy Russia, where there is no place for communist blockheads'.[13]

By contrast, the poetry Nabokov disapproves of is marked by incorrect rhymes, rhythms and accents (which he fastidiously quotes and identifies in each review), and vague or wild imagery. It is, in short, 'careless' (*'nebrezhnyi'*), 'verbose' (*'monogoslovnyi'*), 'illiterate' (*'bezgramotnyi'*), and 'incomprehensible' (*'bezotvestvennyi'*). No eighteenth-century stickler for poetic decorum could be more unbending than the young Nabokov of these reviews; a comparison can be made with T. S. Eliot's criticism from the 1920s, with its equally anxious defence of the very rules of taste that he – like Nabokov – was, arguably, infringing in his own art.[14] Like Eliot, Nabokov was also, however, quick to condemn poetry which, though correct, was boring, and, conversely, to recognize the value of poetic freedom: a full-scale attack on Pasternak's 'incomprehensibility' is tempered by the clear acknowledgement of his talent with which the review begins; while in Vladislav Khodasevich, Nabokov identifies a 'wild, intelligent, shameless freedom plus correct (that is, in a certain sense unfree) rhythm'.[15]

Even in Nabokov's earliest poems, an air of conventionality masks subtleties which would later unfold into those of his mature writing. The very first poem printed here, 'Music', written in that summer of 1914 when Nabokov first took to verse, may seem frigid and juvenile. A fountain sparkles at midnight, and dragonflies hover around it; their sparkling counterpoints its play. Dmitri Nabokov's ornate translation does as much justice as can be done to the poem's ritualized vocabulary. Yet, as so often with such Symbolist period pieces, the implications of the imagery are bolder than they might at first seem. Nabokov's fountain is a symbol of the imagination: of its ceaseless self-replenishing vitality; of its independence from 'the crowd' and political pressure; of its power, in the face of the 'everyday nighttime' of ordinary existence, to gather together 'mirages of lands undescribed', 'mirages of love and of loss'. This fountain, in which the undescribed is realized, and the lost re-found and re-made, can dissolve 'the sinister shade', and by doing so make a new reality play and sparkle into being. In short, in this adolescent fountain already glisten traces of the ideas which Nabokov would elaborate into his great novels, most of all *Pale Fire*, in which the poet John Shade's epiphany of a possible transcendental realm is symbolized by another sparkling fountain. And in surrounding the fountain by dragonflies, Nabokov made an image he would later reuse in the scene of *Lolita* in which Humbert and Quilty sit out on a moonlit hotel porch, watching frail moths being drawn fatally into the bright flame of their fascination. It is telling that the key word of the poem, used three times for the fountain's 'plashing', is *'igra'*, or 'play' – a word at the centre of Nabokov's conceptual world, and one whose dangerous temptations he dramatized in *Lolita*.[16]

'Music' is an unexpectedly rediscovered relic of the summer of 1914 described in *Speak, Memory*, but the account Nabokov gives there of his first poem in fact corresponds to 'The Rain Has Flown', the poem of 1917 which he printed first in *Poems and Problems*:

> A moment later my first poem began. What touched it off? I think I know. Without any wind blowing, the sheer weight of a raindrop, shining in parasitic luxury on a cordate leaf, caused its tip to dip, and what looked like a globule of quicksilver performed a sudden glissando down the center vein, and then, having shed its bright load, the relieved leaf unbent.[17]

So, too, 'The Rain Has Flown' takes its substance from its own vaporous atmosphere, and ends with the sudden unexpected appearance of the poem itself, emblematized as a water-drop or 'globule of quicksilver' falling from an overloaded leaf: 'Downward a leaf inclines its tip / and drops from its tip a pearl.' As such, the poem contrasts suggestively with 'Music', the first of many poems Nabokov would write which realize the imagination's power of creating an artificial centre into which all of experience can, for a moment, be concentrated and controlled. This category includes poems as various as 'The Ruler' (1923), in which Nabokov vaunts his sovereignty over the kingdom of his imagination, and 'The Ballad of Longwood Glen' (1957), a deceptively jaunty, even hokey, piece of Americana, in which the disappearance of a florist (suggestively named Art) leads, via the gathering of people looking for him, to the evolution of an inadvertent site of pilgrimage, a secular holy place. 'The Rain Has Flown', on the other hand, makes itself continuous with its atmosphere, and happens in the dissolution of a moment of intensity, whose dwindling rhythms it catches and follows on their descent towards silence. As such it looks forward to poems such as the untitled 1923 piece that begins 'Like pallid dawn, my poetry sounds gently; / my fleeting cadences soon die away', or 'The Refrigerator Awakes' (1942), in which the poem holds with desperate pity onto the sounds of a refrigerator at night, as it processes its *volatile liquid*' before 'collapsing at last in the criminal / night' of sleep, oblivion, and death (the refrigerator is imagined as a giant trying to die).

In the refrigerator's momentary, saving, transformation of water into frost, or snow, before allowing it again to die back to ephemeral liquidity, Nabokov found a metaphor, as whimsical as it is apt, for the metamorphoses of his own poetry. Like the Georgians he read at Cambridge, Nabokov returned again and again in his poems to rain and snow, so much so that we could say of his poems what he said about Rupert Brooke's in his long 1922 essay on the poet, that 'a love for everything streaming, babbling, lightly-freezing'[18] is expressed in them. And, as with Brooke and other Georgians such as Walter de la Mare and Edward Thomas, this feeling for rain and snow is part of an aesthetic of childhood. In 'Snow' (1930), the poet, trying – as so often – to fall asleep, hears outside his window the crunch of someone walking across packed snow. The sound inspires the Proustian memory of a childhood sled on which he can coast back through the lost years to revisit 'my warmly muffled up, clumsy / childhood'. This poem – like other poems of the late 1920s and early 1930s devoted to childhood – looks forward to the opening chapter of *The Gift*, in which Fyodor has just published a book of poems 'all devoted to a single theme: childhood'. They can easily come across as immature and even mawkish, like Fyodor's poems, a 'miniature verse of charms and chimes'.[19]

Yet by their studied unsophistication they are a defiant actualization of the naïf, that aesthetic ideal of wholeness untroubled by the complex fluttering of the external world, and innocent of the subtle defences that worldly danger may elicit or even force out of us – the aesthetic, in fact, of *Speak, Memory*, with its 'sense of security, of well-being' in which 'everything is as it should be, nothing will ever change, nobody will ever die.'[20] The naïve writer insists on his right to create his own world, like the one Nabokov spoke of in an essay of 1942, calling it 'the emphatically and unshakably illogical world which I am advertising as a home for the spirit'.[21]

In this insistence is the hidden link between these faux-naïf poems of childhood, and the very different poems, such as 'The Ruler', 'The Demon' (1924), and 'The Blazon' (1925), in which Nabokov speaks in the humid tones of the Symbolist magus exercising his kingly dominion over words – the shamanic 'wizard' of 'Fame'; the lord of language who speaks in 'An Evening of Russian Poetry', lamenting that 'Beyond the seas where I have lost a scepter, / I hear the neighing of my dappled nouns'; and the lunatic (or poet) who rants in 'The Madman' (1933). Though merely 'A street photographer in laic life', he is 'now poet, king, Parnassian autocrat', and the moon and trees humbly beg admission into his verse. Here we find the idea of *Pale Fire*, in which Nabokov split these two personae – madman and poet-king – into the two figures of Kinbote and John Shade.

Another group of poems, all of them from before 1925, articulate scenes from Christian iconography – something that will, again, surprise those who know Nabokov from *Lolita* and *Pale Fire*, works whose epiphanies are decidedly aesthetic rather than religious. Such poems include 'The Last Supper' (1920), 'Easter' (1922), 'The Glasses of St Joseph' (1923), and 'The Mother' (1925). The issue of the young Nabokov's relation to Christianity, or faith more generally, is complex and disputed. As we have already seen, in his introduction to *Poems and Problems* Nabokov insisted that the apparently religious quality of some of his early verse was no more than a 'Byzantine' literary style. On the other hand, in her introduction to *Stikhi*, the poet's widow Véra pointed to the 'otherworld' as 'the main theme' in Nabokov, a 'watermark' running through his writing.[22] A sense of the otherworld is, of course, not the same as a commitment to any religious doctrine, but it should be noted that the Christian-sounding poems in this volume form only a small percentage of the many poetic expressions of faith dating from between 1917 and 1925, few if any of which are obviously ironic. At some point around 1923, however, Nabokov began to subsume the intimations of the beyond in his poetry into the iconography of his aestheticism (butterflies, fountains, games). In one interesting untranslated poem of May 1923, not included in this volume, Nabokov declares that we humans 'are the caterpillars of angels',[23] an idea that leads logically to the depictions of butterflies and moths as angels (and demons) in two of the poems published here ('Butterflies' and 'The Hawkmoth', 1926–9 and 1953 respectively) – and to the butterflies which appear, like guardian or witnessing angels, above Lolita and John Shade at moments of peril. Nabokov seems to have moved towards a poetic and spiritual practice closer to that recommended by Gumilev, who in his essay 'Acmeism and the Legacy of Symbolism' (1913) spoke of how his literary school had passed beyond Symbolism's efforts to capture the ineffable in its symbols: 'the principle of Acmeism: remember the existence of the unknowable, always remember it – but do not insult your thinking about it with more or less likely guesses . . . angels, and demons, and elemental and other spirits are now simply part of the material with which the artist works.'[24]

One of the first references to the 'otherworld' comes in the essay on Brooke, where Nabokov characteristically casts the beyond in whimsical terms, drawing at one point on 'Heaven' (1913), Brooke's humorous poem about faith, in which fish imagine the beyond as an 'Eternal Brook' ruled over by an 'Almighty Fin'. Nabokov says that 'in these lines, in this trembling droplet of water, is reflected the essence of all earthly religions.' And he adds that Brooke 'passionately loves the earth'. Even though Brooke senses that beyond it there follow other novels, the novels of faith, nonetheless 'the splashes of the sun, the cries of the wind, the pricks of the rain' are his 'first love'.[25] For the mature Nabokov, any fascination with the beyond which diminished one's fastidious attention to earthly life would be fatal to both literature and happiness; this is the theme of 'Oculus' (1939), with its concluding argument that a world where 'Gone, in fact, is the break between matter / and eternity' is one depleted of all lovable details: 'who can care / for a world of omnipotent vision, / if nothing is monogrammed there?'[26] The Christ that Nabokov's early poems recommend is the child who taught us to see the beauties of the earth, not to disdain them in favour of a cold heaven – the Christ of 'The Glasses of St Joseph', who picks up his carpenter father's glasses from the workbench

> and touched the airy lenses. Instantly
> a sunny shimmer traversed the world, flashed across distant,
> dreary lands, warming the blind, and cheering the sighted.

If this vision corresponds to any stylistic school, it is not Byzantine, but Dutch realist (consider the poem 'Peter in Holland', 1919), or – still more – Pre-Raphaelite. Indeed the scene closely recalls the famous painting by J. S. Millais *Christ in the House of His Parents* (1849–50), which arrived in the Tate Gallery in London in 1921, when Nabokov was studying in England. This is the form of simplicity – a love of minute earthly detail as evidence of the spirit – which is the most important legacy of these early poems to Nabokov's novels.

Not all of Nabokov's poems from the period before 1925 resemble paintings, but in their simplicity they tend towards fairly static patterns: a single passionate declaration; a small tableau; a breath of prayer. Another poetic principle, however, soon emerged in his criticism, coming to compete with and supersede that of simplicity. This was the view that, as he put it in two reviews from the summer of 1927, 'story is just as essential to a poem as to a novel' and 'the reader must begin with curiosity and finish with excitement. About lyric experience, about trifles, one must tell a story as absorbing as the tale of a journey to Africa.'[27] (The reference to Africa is a signal of the growing importance to Nabokov of Gumilev, who hunted lions in Ethiopia.) So, while in the late 1920s Nabokov was developing novels whose prose was as linguistically rich as poetry, he was, at the same time, as he tells us in the introduction to *Poems and*

Problems, trying 'to illustrate the principle of making a short poem contain a plot and tell a story'.

Nabokov's sense of what makes a story was, however, just as subtle, various, and even paradoxical in his verse as it was in his novels. A few poems do tell simple enough stories – 'Lilith' being one which will, notwithstanding Nabokov's vehement denial, remind most readers of the plot of his most famous novel.[28] In most cases, however, the story is made out of such wispy materials as memory, dream, or inspiration – or all three at once – and as such its artifice is left perfectly apparent. Some poems tell the story of their own making, like 'The Skater' (1925), where, at the end of an exquisitely worked sonnet about a figure-skater, we realize that we have all the time been experiencing the tracing out of an equivalent poetic pattern: 'I left behind a single verbal figure, / an instantly unfolding flower, inked.' In 'The Train Wreck' (1925), the movement of the train is the vehicle for that artistic 'defamiliarization' beloved by Nabokov, and the formalist critics such as Viktor Shklovsky who influenced him so much – an unsettling procedure which Nabokov always recognized as a destructive form of beauty: 'objects that have grown demented / awaken in the dark and clunk'. In 'Spring', also from 1925, the train of the poem performs a gentler office to the world, not shaking it to ruin but merely inverting it – 'A crowd of tree trunks, shying, nimbly / goes scurrying up the incline' – a nice image of the action of memory as, at the end of the poem, the train allows the poet to return to his lost house in lost Russia: 'From exile's lamentations distanced, / lives on my every reminiscence / in an inverted quietude'. In these, as in other cases, the train serves as an ironic icon of narrative drive – as if, in a close-up photograph, the only clue that it was a model train, and not a real one, were that the train had painted onto it the image of another train. In another group of poems – the two entitled 'Dream' and 'The Dream' (1926 and 1927, respectively), and 'The Execution' (1927) – a fixed set of images (a dream revenant, an alarm clock, a gun) are rearranged in various patterns, but in every case the hidden principle of the poem is that, in fact, the violent energy of narrative (the clock is a gun) needs to be allowed to spend itself; only then can the illogic of dream and memory find the space and peace to do its (dream-)work.

Nabokov's desire to bring story to poem harks back to his beloved Pushkin, who in *Eugene Onegin* (1832) had written a complete novel in verse. Using the intricate stanzaic pattern of *Onegin*, Nabokov in 1926 wrote his own novella in verse, *The University Poem*. The poem is about the ennui of Nabokov's years as an undergraduate at Cambridge, a sense of marking time that is transferred onto the figure of Violet, the somewhat older girl with whom the protagonist is conducting a half-hearted romance. Nabokov's writing is usually so powerfully energetic, in thought, humour, image, voice, and plot, that it valuably disorients one's idea of him to read Dmitri Nabokov's translation of *The University Poem*, which fully conveys the listlessness of the tale – though the secret of the poem is, surely, Nabokov's ability to cherish all his memories, even those which, by their dull humiliations, might have been expected to make him squeamish. What the reader without Russian is missing, however, is the studied contrast the poem sustains between the prosaic boredom of its subject matter, and the virtuosity of the *Onegin* stanza – fourteen lines, in iambic tetrameter, rhyming *ababccddeffegg*. Fortunately, though, the effect of that stanza is easily accessible, since Nabokov reproduced it in the two brilliant stanzas of his 'On Translating "Eugene Onegin"' (1955), and also memorably described it in his commentary on *Onegin*: 'the opening pattern (a clean-cut sonorous elegiac quatrain) and the terminal one (a couplet resembling the code of an octave or that of a Shakespearean sonnet) can be compared to the patterns on a painted ball or top that are visible at the beginning and at the end of the spin.'[29] This pattern serves Nabokov to capture the poem's alternate focussing and diffraction of memory, which he identifies in Stanzas 12 and 13 – 'something in my memory flashing, / as if unfocussed, and then clearer / only to vanish once again' – before the vanished image is found again: 'There! Now it's in focus. Now I see clearly. / It's there, the satiny-chestnut iridescent glimmer / of her coiffure'. 'Focus' is meant literally, for the image Nabokov is deploying is of memory as a microscope bringing slides of the past in and out of focus, something he had done as a young student of Biology at Cambridge (he switched to studying literature), and which he describes in Stanza 11: 'To twist a screw of brass, / so that, in the water's droplets, / the world would radiantly appear / minute – that is what occupied my day.' Such focussing and unfocussing enacts not only memory but the poem's sense of the ceaseless and unfixable mobility of life: as, in its final lines, Nabokov bids farewell to the muse that had presided over *The University Poem*, and supplicates her patronage for his protean vision of the world:

> cherishing each instant,
> blessing each motion,
> do not allow it to freeze still,
> perceive the delicate rotation
> of the slightly tilted earth.

In his introduction to *Stikhotvoreniia*, Nabokov said of another such invocation, the poem titled simply 'The Muse' (1929), that it 'marks the end of the period of my youthful creativity'.[30] But it not only marks that end, it also dramatizes it, and as such it inaugurates a new phase of Nabokov's writing in which the loss of his younger lyric self would become the subject and condition of his poetry, and its fundamental issue the shifting 'infinite subdivisions'[31] (Gumilev's phrase) of the human personality. 'The Muse' begins by invoking the muse of the poem's title in stately tones ('Your coming I recall'), but by the end she has become an old country neighbour, at once familiar, distant, and disenchanted. In 'How I Love You' (1934), she is merely 'You', a slippery, vanishing pronoun, unlocatable in any sane landscape, and needing to be defended from those who would recognize and articulate her; the poem breathlessly zigzags between wanting to catch and hold that 'you' and wishing to leave it free. In many of the other poems of the 1930s where Nabokov makes a 'you' out of his younger lyric self and then addresses it, he leaves the pronoun loose and unspecified enough for the reader to feel as if he or she too is being addressed, uncomfortably inhabiting some facet of another's subjectivity, as in a bewildering dream. 'At Sunset' (1935) begins: 'At sunset, by the same bench, / as in the days of my youth, // At sunset, you know the kind,' before subtly altering that 'you' from the pronoun casually invoked to support lazy suppositions of shared experience ('you know the kind') to a very different 'you', now the formal subject of the unconscious being directed to re-enact a privately evolved ritual of incomplete mourning: 'As then, in those distant days, / smile and avert your face, // If to souls of those long dead / it is given sometimes to return.' Elsewhere, as in 'We So Firmly Believed' (1938), the relations between 'you, my youth' and the 'I' which speaks are specified – 'You've long ceased to be I' – but, as if to compensate, 'we' is unmoored. Though in the title and the opening line it resounds with a comfortable pre-modernist assumption of a shared community of belief, the reader soon baulks at that presumption, so alien to the thinking of a poem which treats 'the linkage of life' as 'rather like a wave's haze / between me and you'.

The play of self is, of course, fundamental to Nabokov's fiction. At the end of *The Real Life of Sebastian Knight* (1941), for instance, the narrator says about his possibly imaginary half-brother Sebastian: 'I am Sebastian, or Sebastian is I, or perhaps we both are someone whom neither of us knows';[32] while in *Pale Fire*, Nabokov conjures up a three-dimensional system of correspondence and contrast describing every possible gradation of personality between his imaginary protagonists, Shade and Kinbote. Such games with identity can be traced back at least as far as 'A Trifle' (1926), in which Nabokov surveys his lived and merely possible selves, collectively signified by the trifling designation of the name which soars above those ill-assorted personae like a mast above the passengers of a cruise-ship. In this poem Nabokov insists on the distinction between his public mask, his selves, and his life. Elsewhere, however, the contrast he most wanted to draw was that between the man and the artist. As he wrote in *Nikolai Gogol* (1944): 'It was the shadow of Gogol that lived his real life – the life of his books, and in them he was an actor of genius.'[33] Two of the early poems in this collection play upon that distinction, 'Shakespeare' (1924) and 'Tolstoy' (1928), both of which explore the seemingly unbridgeable chasm between the merely historical individuals (the Shakespeare who wore a ruff and lived in pubs, the Tolstoy who banged on about village schools) and the 'monstrous genius' hidden behind those masks, which created the host of characters, the 'phantasms' echoes' which 'still vibrate for us' and which endow the authors' names with the fame that should really belong to their nameless genius.

In these poems, it is taken for granted that Shakespeare and Tolstoy's true selves are or will be realized through the ceaseless after-echoes of their art in the minds of their readers – their 'fame'. But in Nabokov's poems of the late 1930s and early 1940s, especially the two long interlinked poems 'Fame' and 'The Paris Poem' of 1942 and 1943 respectively, he took the play of self one stage further by dwelling on his situation as an author in exile, bereaved of his sophisticated Russian émigré readership. 'Fame' declares it is 'addressed to non-beings', and a tormenting voice hectors the poet with his own recognition that whereas literature should fall like 'genuine foliage' on the soil of Russia, 'your unfortunate books // without soil, without path, without ditch, without threshold, / will be shed in a void . . .' Deprived of its native soil, the 'I' of these poems lacks the addressees who could grant it identity and a stage on which to speak; the poet of 'The Paris Poem', addressing the angels hauling away his fellow émigrés, pleads weakly: 'You at least might reflect, you at least might / condescend to glance briefly – Meanwhile / I remain your specterful (signature / illegible. Night. Cloudy sky).'

For much of their length, these spasmodic disjunctive poems give us the self dislimned, a mere 'procession of clouds' and clash of bodiless voices. Personalities and even thoughts are but illusions engineered by the crunching machinery of rhetoric, 'A huge clean sheet of paper I started / to extract from myself', as 'The Paris Poem' puts it. As such, they are closely related to Nabokov's thinking for the book on Gogol he was writing at the same time, in which 'the peripheral characters . . . are engendered by the subordinate clauses of . . . various metaphors, comparisons, and lyrical outbursts', so that 'we are faced by the remarkable phenomenon of mere forms of speech directly giving rise to live creatures.'[34] Some such figure enters at the beginning of 'Fame', 'a character, / waxlike, lean-loined, with red nostrils soot-stuffed', who is 'just garrulous dust', the residue of an adverb, like Akaky Akakievich, the protagonist of Gogol's 'The Overcoat' (1842). These poems are, like 'The Overcoat' in Nabokov's description, 'a grotesque and grim nightmare making black holes in the dim pattern of life'[35] – as is the Gogolian novel Nabokov would publish in 1947, *Bend Sinister*. Or they would be, were it not for the fact that, unlike *Bend Sinister*, Nabokov in these poems still credits, and vindicates, the power of his own lyric voice to make its own audience, grant its own authority, and forge its own bridges across those black holes in the texture of life and language – as in 'Fame':

> But my word, curved to form an aerial viaduct,
> spans the world, and across in a strobe-effect spin
> of spokes I keep endlessly passing incognito
> into the flame-licked night of my native land.

It is startling to turn from these Russian poems, their surfaces pocked and rutted by doubt, to the ones in English that Nabokov was writing at the same time, poems which hurtle forwards across intricate metrical patterns with an unhesitating confidence that seems both artistic and social. In 'A Literary Dinner' (1942), for instance, we glimpse the poet at a dinner party, silently storing up the banal chatter as material for future satire, an impassive predator let loose on a roomful of his innocently pompous prey – a figure reminiscent of the cruel mimic who narrates *Pnin* (1957). In 'An Evening of Russian Poetry', Nabokov adopts a more benign but no less invulnerable persona, as the guest lecturer at a girls' college, whose talk is as smooth as a magician's patter, and so deftly powerful that it can incorporate the girls' questions into its forward-moving rhythms as easily as the carnivore of 'A Literary Dinner' can eat up the sentences he is offered.

Yet, just as there are stretches of 'Fame' and 'The Paris Poem' in which the debris of broken phrases suddenly joins together to form an aerial viaduct, so, conversely, the apparently smooth surface of Nabokov's English poems conceals various trap-doors, such as the moment at the end of 'An Evening of Russian Poetry' when the good-night bidden to the speaker is revealed, in translation, as an augury of the tortured insomnia that awaits him. That moment looks forward to *Pale Fire*, in which Nabokov establishes an apparently absolute contrast between his two protagonists – the unhappy, errant Russian exile, Kinbote, and John Shade, the sunny New England poet, who still lives in the house he was born in – only to undermine it by indicating a series of affinities so intricate that many readers have been led to believe Shade and Kinbote are two opposite facets of the same person. Bringing this thought to bear on Nabokov's English poems raises a series of questions. Is the satirist of 'A Literary Dinner' really at home in his surroundings, or is his aggression the imperfectly masked expression of his vulnerability, his hunger the cousin to that hunger for death of the giant heard crying out all through 'the criminal / night' of 'The Refrigerator Awakes'? Is the voice which gallops through these poems the well-tuned instrument of the poet's will, or does it belong more to the bully who hectors him at the beginning of 'Fame', 'like an evil old schoolmate', so that the poet is reduced to a listener, an 'eavesdropping self' as he calls it in 'Exile' (1942), defenceless against the alien voices which torment him – not least that strange accent he has learned to hear coming from his own mouth? The poet who seems so confident of his place in the world and his sense of timing is capable of exclaiming, in 'Restoration' (1952): 'To think that any fool may tear / by chance the web of when and where.' What raises the English poems above mere lightness is, then, that their apparently seamless surfaces yield on examination to disclose many such Gogolian tears in the fabric of consciousness, like the 'howling hole' out of which 'a one-legged child that howled with laughter' comes hopping in the nightmare of 'Dream' (1944).

As such Nabokov's poems in English realize, as fully as *Pale Fire* later would, Nabokov's insight that 'the evolution of sense is the evolution of nonsense'[36] (the dictum of a character in *Pnin*); that the rich meaningfulness of a particular language is a fragile miracle which depends on an almost infinite root-system of hidden half-meanings; and that that dense network, the source of poetry and dream alike, is ignored only at the risk of madness or despair. As long ago as 1924, in his prose poem 'Russian River' (not included in this volume), Nabokov had imagined those half-meanings as the pearly babble of a river; the poet standing on the bridge of a foreign city is reproached by the river passing beneath him for having forgotten it.[37] This underground current of sound and meaning recurs through the

poems, sometimes as a river, sometimes as a wind – and some-
times as the murmur of the sea tides, as in 'Soft Sound' (1926).
In 'An Evening of Russian Poetry', Nabokov returns to the
image of 'Russian River', declaring that 'most rivers use a kind
of rapid Russian, / and so do children talking in their sleep.' A
language's meanings reach all the way through its surrounding
world, so that a language *is* a world. The point is implicit in all
metafictive literature, but Nabokov whimsically enlarges it
through the conceit that not only the images and metaphors but
even the alphabets of Russian (and Greek) were modelled on
the features of their native landscapes. Elsewhere in the poem,
Nabokov gives the point more substance by showing how the
different rhymes available in Russian and English predispose
the mind to make different connections and distinctions, so that
in Russian

> love automatically rhymes with blood,
> nature with liberty, sadness with distance,
> humane with everlasting, prince with mud,
> moon with a multitude of words, but sun
> and song and wind and life and death with none.

Those lost rhymes and missing metaphors are the 'false shadows'
that 'track me as I pass', the agents of the world the poet has
tried (and failed) to abandon.

   This metatextual predisposition of Nabokov to see world as
word and the universe as alphabetical (as he says in 'Fame', 'in
place of the stars I put letters') can be traced all the way back to
the early 1920s: to 'Cubes' (1924), for instance, in which he
declares that 'in this eerie, alien world, / letters of life, and whole
lines, / have been transposed by the typesetters.' In America,
though, Nabokov began to work in the medium of *New Yorker*
light verse (as also practised by friends and admirers such as
John Updike and his Cornell colleague Morris Bishop), a medium
whose basic strategy is to grasp the world linguistically, through
snippets of chit-chat, misheard phrases, and odd extracts from
newspapers. As Updike would later write in the introduction to
his *Collected Poems*, serious poetry derives from 'the real (the
given, the substantial) world, light verse from the man-made

world of information – books, newspapers, words, signs'.[38] So, 'The Refrigerator Awakes' incorporates informational blurbs about how refrigerators work, Polar expeditions, and kitchen advertising; 'An Evening of Russian Poetry' takes as its epigraph an extract from a letter which the speaker has, supposedly, received; and in 'Ode to a Model' (1955), the poet descants on his pursuit of a model through all the magazine advertisements in which she has appeared.

It is impossible fully to appreciate Nabokov's American poetry, including the poem in *Pale Fire*, unless one recognizes that it plays with and deepens light verse. We have the singsong couplets and pedestrian phrasing of 'The Ballad of Longwood Glen' ('That Sunday morning, at half past ten, / Two cars crossed the creek and entered the glen') and 'The Poplar' (1952) ('Before this house a poplar grows / Well versed in dowsing, I suppose'); the scoutmaster brightness of the triplets in 'Lines Written in Oregon' (1953) ('Esmerelda! Now we rest / Here, in the bewitched and blest / Mountain forests of the West'); and the ponderous processing of a sci-fi conceit through the mechanical quatrains of 'Voluptates Tactionum' (1951) ('Some inevitable day / On the editorial page / Of your paper it will say, / "Tactio has come of age"'). The rhymes unfailingly have the naïve-seeming heaviness of verse for children – after all, as Nabokov says in 'An Evening of Russian Poetry', 'the rhyme is the line's birthday, as you know'. Sometimes, though, one birthday is not enough, and Nabokov yields to the temptation of rhyme within the line, producing a still more childlike ringing: as in 'A Poem' (1942), the elegy in which Nabokov likens the prostrate body of a dead US soldier to a small child who has fallen over:

> When he was small, when he would fall,
> on sand or carpet he would lie
> quite flat and still until he knew
> what he would do: get up or cry.

Or a poem will, with a new stanza, pick up a new subject like a new toy, with a bright confidence in its ability to restart itself that is also characteristic of light verse. So, in 'Restoration', the poet's account of his daughter's nightmare is immediately interrupted by his description of a party trick about 'a poet who can strip / a William Tell or Golden Pip / in one uninterrupted peel'. This self-distracting inconsequence is one of the main devices in Shade's 'Pale Fire', where it consistently infiltrates the poem with a thread of bathos: in the very first stanza, Shade has no sooner established the image of himself as 'the shadow of the waxwing slain' than he undercuts his epic rhetoric by chirpily declaring: 'And from the inside, too, I'd duplicate / Myself, my lamp, an apple on a plate.'[39] Conversely, Nabokov often plays with the possibilities for sentimentality afforded by the incongruous lists that light verse delights in, as in the list of things to which the poet has said goodbye in 'Softest of Tongues' – furnished flats, streets, sky-writing, hidden designs, banana skins, waiters, cuts, love. This essentially simple trick for making fragile poetic possession out of loss was brought to the highest level of art by another *New Yorker* writer, Elizabeth Bishop, in her famous poem 'One Art' ('lost door keys'; 'my mother's watch'; 'two cities, lovely ones').[40] John Shade, a much less gifted writer than Bishop, somewhat overuses the device, in a way that Nabokov intends to be telling about his personal as well as artistic limitations – specifically, he is far too complacent about being able to organize the disarray of loss into the easy landscape of a cute rhetorical figure: 'And our best yesterdays are now foul piles / Of crumpled names, phone numbers and foxed files.'[41]

But Nabokov was a better poet than Shade, and what gives power to the tinkling or breezy surface of his English verse is his ability to press, twist, or tear the top-weave of civilized sense to reveal holes and snarls beneath. One of his simplest tricks is to drop a letter, so that the civilized aggression of 'A Literary Dinner' is revealed by the poet pretending to mishear an invitation to 'meet' his fellow guests as an encouragement to 'eat' them. So, too, in *Pnin*, it takes the change of only a single letter to reveal in Pnin's name, the object of much supposedly good-humoured mockery from Americans who cannot pronounce it, the deep-buried pain of a man stripped of dignity by exile. In 'Exile', Nabokov expertly manages his unusual mixed amphibrachic metre so that the beat seems to keep interrupting itself with a complicated cross-rhythm that the ear can never quite accustom itself to, with the effect that the poem seems to be making tears and gaps in its fabric at the very same time as it is weaving it, like the 'blue holes' that the wind makes:

> . . . in the waterproof gloss
> of college-bred poplars that rustle and toss
> their slippery shadows at pied
> young beauties, all legs, as they bicycle through
> his shoulder, his armpit, his heart, and the two
> big books that are hurting his side.

The gawky enjambments are, like the shadows of internal off-rhyme (heart/hurt), essential to the effect of giddy despair – as, too, in 'The Refrigerator Awakes', written the same year, with its 'giant / waking up in the torture house, trying to die / and not dying, and trying / not to cry and immediately crying'. In 'Ode to a Model', Nabokov plays a series of intricate games with off-rhyme, incomplete rhyme, and reversed rhyme, all to disturb the false harmonies of the sham world of advertising and mass-produced beauty: the 'model' is brought straight down to earth by being 'rhymed' in the first stanza with 'sod'; her 'armpit', in the next stanza, is 'pitiful' though her 'eyelash' is 'stylish'. By the fourth stanza, the ear can scarcely tell which false or parodic rhymes to match: 'parody', 'cherry tree', 'parapet', 'archery'. Against the unanswering world of the magazine, with its false aesthetic of simple harmony and proportion, the poet can do no more than fire technical questions: ' "Can one – somebody asked – / rhyme 'star' and 'disaster'?" / . . . Can one marry a model? / Kill your past, make you real, raise a family / by removing you bodily / from back numbers of Sham?'

But if Nabokov's English poems merely twisted and satirized the patterns and orders of his social world, they would be much less interesting than they are. Though they do justice to the underground stream of nonsense and nightmare, they do so without draining all meaning from the visible world, and they resound with the recognition that John Shade comes to in *Pale Fire* when, thinking he has found someone else who shared his near-death vision of a fountain, he is disappointed to discover that it was in fact a mountain, transfigured by a typo in the article he had read. Again, life turns on a single letter, yet for Shade this is not a prescription for despair: 'But all at once it dawned on me that *this* / Was the real point, the contrapuntal theme; / . . . Yes! It sufficed that I in life could find / Some kind of link-and-bobolink, some kind / Of correlated pattern in the game'. That is, it is enough for 'A feeling of fantastically planned, / Richly rhymed life' to be achieved through language and art, precarious, fragile, and artificial though that achieved feeling may be. 'And if my private universe scans right, / So does the verse of galaxies divine / Which I suspect is an iambic line.'[42]

Nabokov had put the point somewhat more directly in 'Restoration'. Although, on the one hand, 'any fool may tear / by chance the web of when and where', this truth need only be inverted for us to see 'that every brain is on the brink / of nameless bliss no brain can bear'. The alliteration, humorously exaggerated, makes the web, and puts us on the brink between sense and nonsense. And it is characteristic of these poems that, in rhyming 'tear' and 'where', Nabokov gives an emphatic substantiality to a small connective word ('where') which a 'serious' poet would be embarrassed to rhyme. The rhymes of the world created in these poems are not the grand ones of the world Nabokov mourned in 'An Evening of Russian Poetry' – love and blood, nature and liberty, sadness and distance. Rather, they are the two wistful ways of saying goodbye in 'Softest of Tongues': 'that's that' and 'wave . . . your hat'; or 'sooner' and 'lunar' in the web of 'Dream'; or the eerily self-mirroring couplets of 'The Poplar' (1952) – 'grows' and 'suppose', 'chair' and 'there', 'me' and 'tree'. The poem makes us realize how fragile and contingent are the meanings of even 'there' and 'me'. Such tiny words, which place the fragile 'me' in the home of a 'there', are not to be taken for granted, any more than the connections offered to a lonely dying exiled poet in 'The Room' (1950), who finds beside his bed two sacred books of connections, the Bible and the Telephone Directory, 'the Book / of Heaven and the Book of Bell'. For the poet writing this poem – whose 'line' rhymes with 'mine' – 'I' rhymes with 'die'. Indeed, as he later argues, 'A poet's death is, after all, / a question of technique, a neat / enjambment, a melodic fall.' But so is a poet's – or anyone's – life; and as such life, with all its connectedness, is open, still, to restoration in art:

> And here a life had come apart
> in darkness, and the room had grown
> a ghostly thorax, with a heart
> unknown, unloved – but not alone.

Thomas Karshan, 2012

NOTES

1. Vladimir Nabokov, *Speak, Memory* (London: Penguin, 2000), p. 167.
2. Vladimir Nabokov, *Poems and Problems* (New York: McGraw-Hill, 1970), p. 13. (Henceforth abbreviated as *PP*.)
3. At the first mention of a poem in this introduction, its date has been included in brackets. As in this instance, the date is generally the date of composition; where that is not known, however, the publication date has been given instead. For fuller detail about the publication history of each poem, please refer to the notes at the end of this volume.
4. *PP*, pp. 13–15.
5. Vladimir Nabokov, *Strong Opinions* (New York: McGraw-Hill, 1973).
6. See G. S. Smith, 'Notes on Prosody', and Barry Scherr, 'Poetry', in *The Garland Companion to Vladimir Nabokov*, edited by Vladimir Alexandrov (New York: Garland, 1995), pp. 561–6 and 608–25. As Scherr (p. 612), sums it up:

> Nabokov's poetry is quite conservative in its use of forms ... Beginning to write during a time when many poets were using meters other than the conventional binary (iambic and trochaic) or ternary (anapests, amphibrachs, and dactyls), Nabokov instead largely followed the practice of his beloved nineteenth-century predecessors. His poetry is largely iambic, and among the iambic measures he shows a strong preference for the tetrameter ... Nabokov also shows a strong preference for the more traditional exact rhyme, making only occasional use of the approximate

rhyme found in much poetry of his day. He is equally conservative in his choice of stanzaic forms, overwhelmingly favoring quatrains rhyming AbAb.

7. David Rampton, 'The Art of Invocation: The Role of Apostrophe in Nabokov's Early Poetry', *Russian Literature Triquarterly* 24 (1991), pp. 341–54 (p. 345).
8. Vladimir Nabokov, *Lolita* (London: Penguin, 1980), pp. 9, 307.
9. Vladimir Nabokov, *Stikhi* (Ardis: Ann Arbor, 1979), pp. 80–81.
10. *Speak, Memory*, p. 205.
11. Vladimir Nabokov, *Nikolai Gogol* (New York: New Directions, 1961), p. 55.
12. Vladimir Nabokov, *Sobranie sochinenii russkogo perioda* (*Collected Works of the Russian Period*), 5 vols. (St Petersburg: Symposium, 1999–2000), vol. 1, p. 744. (Henceforth abbreviated as *SS*.)
13. Ibid., vol. 2, p. 644.
14. I borrow this comparison from Alexander Dolinin, who first made it in a lecture given at the Nabokov Museum in St Petersburg in the summer of 2001.
15. *SS*, vol. 2, pp. 641, 638–9, 650.
16. On this point, see my book, Thomas Karshan, *Vladimir Nabokov and the Art of Play* (Oxford: Oxford University Press, 2011).
17. *Speak, Memory*, p. 168.
18. *SS*, vol. 1, p. 729.
19. Vladimir Nabokov, *The Gift* (London: Weidenfeld & Nicolson, 1963), pp. 16, 22.
20. *Speak, Memory*, p. 62.
21. Vladimir Nabokov, 'The Creative Writer', *Bulletin of the New England Modern Languages Association* 1 (January 1942), pp. 21–9 (p. 22). A version of this essay appears as 'The Art of Literature and Commonsense' in Nabokov's *Lectures on Literature* (San Diego: Harcourt, 1980), pp. 371–81.
22. *Stikhi*, p. i.
23. Ibid., p. 105.
24. Nikolai Gumilev, *Selected Works of Nikolai S. Gumilev*, selected and translated by Burton Raffel and Alla Burago (Albany, NY: SUNY Press, 1972), pp. 247–8.
25. *SS*, vol. 1, p. 734.
26. We can see this theme of the need to recognize and love the divinity of the earth anticipated in various poems from 1920–21, such as '*I. A. Buninu*' ('To I. A. Bunin'), which praises Bunin's love for various elements of the earth; '*Razgoraetsia vys*''

('A Peak Flames Up'), in which Nabokov instructs his spirit to recognize that 'quiet God, secret God' lives everywhere in the world, an expression of pantheism; and '*V raiu*' ('In Heaven'), in which Nabokov, having greeted death, decides to turn back and be an earthly poet (*Stikhi*, pp. 38, 39, 40).

27. *SS*, vol. 2, pp. 640, 639–40.
28. For that denial, see Nabokov's footnote on 'Lilith', reprinted as an endnote in this volume (p. 188).
29. Alexander Pushkin, *Eugene Onegin*, translated with a commentary by Vladimir Nabokov, 4 vols. (New York: Bollingen, 1964), vol. 1, p. 10.
30. Vladimir Nabokov, *Stikhotvoreniia 1929–1951* (Paris: Rifma, 1952), n.p.: author's introduction.
31. *Selected Works of Nikolai S. Gumilev*, p. 231.
32. Vladimir Nabokov, *The Real Life of Sebastian Knight* (London: Penguin, 2001), p. 173.
33. *Nikolai Gogol*, p. 26.
34. Ibid., p. 78.
35. Ibid., p. 140.
36. Vladimir Nabokov, *Pnin* (London: Penguin, 2000), p. 27.
37. *SS*, vol. 1, pp. 746–7.
38. John Updike, *Collected Poems 1953–1993* (New York: Alfred A. Knopf, 2003), p. xxiii.
39. Vladimir Nabokov, *Pale Fire* (London: Penguin, 2000), ll. 5–6.
40. Elizabeth Bishop, *Complete Poems* (London: Chatto & Windus, 2004), p. 178.
41. *Pale Fire*, ll. 521–2.
42. Ibid., ll. 806–7, 811–14, 969–70, 974–7.

Collected Poems

Poems Translated by
Dmitri Nabokov

Music

Midst everyday nighttime, there sparkles
a fountain harmonious and high;
it plashes, it quivers, convoking
mirages of lands undescribed.

Around it there noiselessly hover,
immerged in its silvery spray,
dragonflies, their wings in a sparkling
counterpoint to the magic display.

The fountain, loftily floating
its wondrous, its silvery voice,
plashes, and quivers, convoking
mirages of love and of loss.

Undisturbed the dragonflies hover,
like diamonds sparkle their wings,
encircled by snowy-white roses
that follow the font as it sings.

Midst everyday nighttime, there sparkles
a music with billowing might,
that plays like a fountain harmonious
o'er the crowd's noisome, philistine plight.

With its delicate plashing the fountain
has dissolved the sinister shade –
the dragonflies' counterpoint mounting
were sparse echoes now-sparkling souls made.

Revolution

I found a lengthy word with a non-Russian ending,
unwittingly, inside a children's storybook,
and turned away from it with a strange kind of shudder.

That word contained the writing of mysterious passions:
the growls, the howls, the whistles and the senseless visions,
assassinated horses' vitreous eyes,

the sinuous streets, the evil-auguring constructions,
a man, incarnadine, prostrate upon his back,
the bestial motions of somebody's avid hands!

And, once upon a time, how sweet I used to find it
to read of funny rabbits who would dance in spring
with guinea pigs on stumps beneath the moon!

But now the fateful word above my childhood tales,
storm-like, has rushed! Gone is their old simplicity;
and terrifying thoughts, during the doomful nights,

now crepitate like gray newspaper sheets!

Peter in Holland

Out of Muscovy's fierce rigor
He crossed hither in one stride.
To roaring seas he took a liking,
And to our tile-clad little town;

All along the shores he wandered,   5
Sunburnt, rough-hewn, full of youth.
Wind. The ashen-tinted dunes.
The thudding of some axes yonder.

The motley colors of the patchwork
Of sails upon the rippled seas.   10
A flock of gulls, the heav'nly vault,
Greenish, like a faience glaze.

Evenings passed in discourse sage.
Tankards. Somnolent companions.
Reveries in tones victorious   15
Summoned carpenter-tsar Peter.

He pondered gravely at the table,
And the clock distinctly ticked.
I recall: his coarse mustache,
The resolute and fearless gaze,   20

Shadows cast by head and elbows,
The shelving of the little tavern,
On the stove the evening's shimmer,
And a pattern of blue squares.

The Last Supper

The hour is pensive, the supper severe,
the predictions are treason and parting.
The nocturnal pearl bathes with its light
the petals of the oleander.

Apostle inclines toward apostle.
The Christ has silvery hands.
The candles pray lucidly, and on the table
creep the winged insects of night.

Easter

For his father's death

I see a radiant cloud, I see a rooftop glisten
like a mirror, far away . . . I listen
to breathing shade, light's stillicide . . .
You're absent – why? You're dead, and on a day
the humid world is bluish. God's sacred spring is on her way,   5
    swelling, calling . . . And you've died.

And yet, if every stream anew the wonder sings,
and yet, if every falling golden thaw-drop rings –
if these are not bedazzling lies,
but quivering, dulcet convocations: 'Rise again' –   10
a mighty 'Blossom!', then you are in this refrain,
    you're in this splendor, you're alive! . . .

The Ruler

An India invisible I rule:
　　come 'neath the azure of my realm,
I shall command my naked wizard
　　to change a snake into a bracelet for thee.

To thee, O princess who defies description,
　　I offer, for a kiss, Ceylon:
and, for thy love, my whole, luxuriant, ancient,
　　star-weighty firmament.

My peacock and my panther, velvet-sheeny,
　　both languish: 'round the palace,
like showers, the palmy copses patter:
　　we're waiting, all of us, to see thy face.

I'll give thee earrings, twin teardrops of sunrise,
　　I'll give the heart out of my breast.
I'm emperor, and if you don't believe it,
　　then don't – but come in any case.

The Glasses of St Joseph

Wipe off your teardrops and listen: One sunny midday,
    an aged
carpenter forgot his glasses on his workbench. Laughing,
a boy ran in; paused; espied; sneaked up;
and touched the airy lenses. Instantly
a sunny shimmer traversed the world, flashed across distant,   5
dreary lands, warming the blind, and cheering the sighted.

Like pallid dawn, my poetry sounds gently:
    my fleeting cadences soon die away,
and it's unlikely that a keen descendent
    will recollect my avian sobriquet.

5   What can I do, my muse, my darling. We shall,
        in footnotes, unpretentiously endure . . .
    I can't sing forth, I can't convey to others
        how much they need to hold God's shadow dear,

    how we can see God's shadow undulating
10   as through our motley curtains it transpires,
    how day and night are precious beakers holding
        life-giving water and sidereal wine.

    I can't sing forth, I can't convey – and, shortly,
        they will forget this pallid dawn of mine,
15 and she who first forgets will be the same one
        on whom the gift of my last rays will shine.

    And yet I am content, my muse – for silence
        and tenderness you are; one can't be sad
    with you; from each day's song the worldly turmoil,
20   like a superfluous syllable, you've banned.

Shakespeare

Amid grandees of times Elizabethan
you shimmered too, you followed sumptuous customs;
the circle of ruff, the silv'ry satin that
encased your thigh, the wedgelike beard – in all of this
you were like other men . . . Thus was enfolded   5
your godlike thunder in a succinct cape.

Haughty, aloof from theater's alarums,
you easily, regretlessly relinquished
the laurels twining into a dry wreath,
concealing for all time your monstrous genius   10
beneath a mask; and yet, your phantasms' echoes
still vibrate for us: your Venetian Moor,
his anguish; Falstaff's visage, like an udder
with pasted-on mustache; the raging Lear . . .
You are among us, you're alive; your name, though,   15
your image, too – deceiving, thus, the world –
you have submerged in your beloved Lethe.
It's true, of course, a usurer had grown
accustomed, for a sum, to sign your work
(that Shakespeare – Will – who played the Ghost in *Hamlet*,   20
who lived in pubs, and died before he could
digest in full his portion of a boar's head) . . .

The frigate breathed, your country you were leaving.
To Italy you went. A female voice
called singsong through the iron's pattern,   25
called to her balcony the tall *inglese*,
grown languid from the lemon-tinted moon
amid Verona's streets. My inclination
is to imagine, possibly, the droll

and kind creator of *Don Quixote*
exchanging with you a few casual words
while waiting for fresh horses – and the evening
was surely blue. The well behind the tavern
contained a pail's pure tinkling sound . . . Reply –
whom did you love? Reveal yourself – whose memoirs
refer to you in passing? Look what numbers
of lowly, worthless souls have left their trace,
what countless names Brantôme has for the asking!
Reveal yourself, god of iambic thunder,
you hundred-mouthed, unthinkably great bard!

No! At the destined hour, when you felt banished
by God from your existence, you recalled
those secret manuscripts, fully aware
that your supremacy would rest unblemished
by public rumor's unashamèd brand,
that ever, midst the shifting dust of ages,
faceless you'd stay, like immortality
itself – then, in the distance, smiling, vanished.

Cubes

Let us fold the wings of our visions.
It's night. Buildings, all angular, on each other
topple. Shadows are fractured.
The street lamp is a broken flame.

In the room a wooden wind inclines   5
the furniture. It's hard for the mirror to retain
the table and the orange-laden tray.
And my face is emerald.

You are a flight, a poem, in your black dress,
of black angles in this motley world.   10
You funereal theorem, you press
your sharp knee against the ceiling.

Good God, in this eerie, alien world,
letters of life, and whole lines,
have been transposed by the typesetters. Let's fold   15
our wings, my lofty angel.

St Petersburg

Come hither, nebulous Leila!
Forsaken spring, to me return!
Sails of pale green, sails that will billow,
the palace gardens will unfurl.

Along their boundary eagles shimmer.
With lazy murmurs the Neva
like Lethe flows. An elbow mark
was left by Pushkin on the granite.

Leila, stop it – that will do,
stop weeping, O my springtime bygone.
Just look what a fine fish, light-blue,
is limned upon that floating signboard.

In Peter's pastel sky all's hushed.
There's a flotilla of aery vapors,
and the octagonal wood paviors
still have their layer of golden dust.

Evening

I heaved from my shoulder my pick and my shovel
    into a corner of the barn,
I dried off my sweat, ambled out to greet sunset,
    a bonfire cool and rosy-hued.

It peacefully blazed beyond towering beeches,   5
    in between funereal boughs,
where fleetingly shimmered ineffable echoes
    of a vibrant nightingale,

and a guttural din, choirs of toads, gutta-percha-like,
    sang resilient on the pond.   10
It broke off. My forehead was trustingly, downily
    brushed by the flight of a passing moth.

The hills grew more somber: there, flashed reassuringly
    a twinkle of nocturnal lights.
In the distance, a train chugged and vanished. A lingering   15
    whistle lingeringly died . . .

The fragrance was grassy. Entranced I stood, thoughtless:
    and, when the nebulous hoot was stilled,
I saw night had fallen, stars hung close above me,
    and tears were streaming down my face.   20

Fortune-telling

On Christmas Eve, toward midnight,
outside the window stood,
reborn, a chopped-down fir copse,
my argentated wood.

5 Amidst the misty moonlight
I found the proper room. -
That candle, my Svetlana,
between mirrors illume.

Across the basin's water
10 the magic flame will float;
accoasts in rapid order
the little nutshell boat.

And in the dusk, where, under
a lustre, melts parquet,
15 let's hear what fortunes utters
our little neighbor gray.

Upon the faded azure
the cards you can prepare . . .
One moment grand-dad's scowling,
20 the next he lifts his brow.

And he picks up and places
funereal-colored spades
upon the diamonds' faces,
of lacquered, orange shade.

That's how it is, Svetlana –
morose grows your regard.
For us, no sham nirvana
is augured by these cards.

I'm not much of a wizard,
the grand-dad's in his grave,
so there is no one, is there,
to question hoary fate.

Immerged in darkening glimmer,
now everything recedes,
the luster's crystal pendants,
the white piano's sheen.

The flame's out in the nutshell . . .
And you are gone for good,
my legendary fir copse,
my argentated wood.

The Demon

Whence have you flown? What is this sorrow you are
    breathing?
Explain to me, why do your lips, O winged one,
seem deathly pale, why are your wings with ocean scented?

The demon answers me: 'You're famished and you're young,
but sounds are not the thing to sate you. Do not touch them,
those strings discordant you yourself have strung.

No music's more sublime than silence. You're created
for unrelenting silence. Recognize its seal
upon a stone, on love, in stars above the roadway.'

He's vanished. Night dissolves. God orders me to sound.

The Skater

He had a muse as his ice-skating teacher,
Terpsichore in winter guise – behold:
his brow is bared, he wears black riding breeches,
upon his chest there burns a medal's gold.

He whirls, and underneath the diamond lightning   5
of his intelligence-defying skate
breaks off its curve and, starlike, widens
the image of a flower ornate.

And thus, upon the ice compact and silky,
a sunflower is outlined. But wait –   10
have I myself, by that melodious whistling,
not flashed before you with a poem's skate?

I left behind a single verbal figure,
an instantly unfolding flower, inked.
And yet tomorrow, vertical and silent,   15
the snow will dust the scribble-scrabbled rink.

Spring

The engine toward the country flies,
A crowd of tree trunks, shying, nimbly
goes scurrying up the incline:
the smoke, like a white billow, mingles
with birches' motley Apriline.
Velour banquettes inside the carriage
of summer covers are still free.
A yellow trackside dandelion
is visited by its first bee.

Where once there was a snowdrift, only
an oblong, pitted isle is left
beside a ditch that's turning verdant;
of springtime smelling, now grown wet,
the snow is overlaid with soot.

The country house is cold and twilit.
The garden, to the joy of doves,
contains a cloud-reflecting puddle.
The columns and the aged roof,
also the elbow of the drainpipe –
there's need of a fresh coat for all,
a pall of green paint; on the wall
the merry shadow of the painter
and the ladder's shadow fall.

The birches' tops in their cool azure,
the country house, the summer days,
are but the same, recurring image,
yet their perfection grows always.
From exile's lamentations distanced,
lives on my every reminiscence

in an inverted quietude:
What's lost forever is immortal;
and this eternity inverted
is the proud soul's beatitude.

Dream

One time, at night, the window-sill
was loudly spattered by the rain.
The Lord his secret dream-book opened,
and chose me his most blissful dream.

Resounding with alarm familiar,
night, loudly sobbing, shook the house.
My dream was a blue-colored roadway
that through a shady hamlet passed.

Beneath the soft mound of the cargo
the wheels creaked, muffled far below:
supine, I rode home from the haying,
and shadows made the cart seem blue.

Again, with ponderous insistence,
at every turning of the dream,
the frame kept creaking and kept listing
as the window breathed with rain.

And I, within my slumber's blueness,
confused reality with dream:
which was that fateful, alien nightline,
the restless moaning of that frame –

and which, amid warm hay, were daisies,
right here, close to my very lips,
and foliated shadows flowing
in ringlike torrents from above . . .

The Train Wreck

'Neath twilight's vault, into the meadows,
enveloped in the toppled smoke,
at full career the cars are heading
behind the engine's fiery glow:

the baggage car, locked tight, foreboding,   5
where trunks are piled on top of trunks,
where objects that have grown demented
awaken in the dark and clunk –

then, in succession, the four sleepers,
the whole row paneled with veneer,   10
whose windows flash like mirrored lightning,
with fleeting, alternating fire.

An early drowsiness makes someone
pull down a leather window blind,
and, 'midst the clattering and crackling,   15
the right refrain acutely finds.

Those not asleep don't take their eyes off
the ceiling's vague concavities,
where swings, beneath dim-filtered lamplight,
the tassel of a sliding shade.   20

A trifling thing – a bolt untightened,
and, suddenly, beneath one's head,
the clinging flange, the speeding iron,
jumps off the evil-fated rail.

And, up and down the nighttime flatland,
the telegraph beats like a heart,
and people hurtle on a handcar,
their lanterns lifted in the dark.

A sorry thing: the night is dewy,
but here there's wreckage, flame, lament . . .
No wonder that the driver's daughter
an eerie dream of ballast dreamt,

in which around the bend came howling
a hurtling multitude of wheels,
and to its doom a pair of angels
a giant locomotive drove.

The first of them who manned the throttle
advanced his lever with a smirk,
as, incandescent feathers gleaming,
he peered into onrushing murk.

The second one, the winged fireman,
with steely, scintillating scales,
untiringly, with blackened shovel,
hurled coal into the firebox blaze.

Ut Pictura Poesis

To M. V. Dobuzhinsky

O recollection, piercing beam,
transfigure my exile,
transfix me, recollection
of Petersburg's clouds, barge-like,
'midst windswept heavenly expanses,   5
of unfrequented back-road fences,
of street lamps with expressions kind . . .
O'er my Neva, there come to mind
those twilights like the rustling
of obliquely shading pencils.   10

All this the smoothly stroking painter
in front of me unfolded, and
I had the sense that only lately
this very wind my face had fanned,
which he'd depicted by the flying   15
autumn leaves, by the untidy clouds,
and down the quay a humming flowed,
the bells in the penumbra dinned –
the cathedral's bronzen swings . . .

What a familiar courtyard stands nearby,   20
what stony posts! If I could only
step across, clamber inside,
stand for a while where snow-banks slumber,
and where logs lie, compactly stacked,
or 'neath the arch on the canal,   25

where on the stony oval, tinted blue,
shimmer fortress and Neva.

A Trifle

A trifle – a mast's denomination, plans – trailed
by a seagull, soars my life;
and, on the deck, a man, lap-robed,
inhales the radiance – it is I.

5   I see, upon a glossy postcard,
a bay's depravity of blue
and, white-toothed, a townlet with a retinue
of countless palms, and the abode in which I dwell.

At that same instant, with a cry, I'll show you
10   myself, myself – but in a different town:
like a parrot snapping with its beak,
I scrabble at the scrapbook with its cards.

That one – that's me, with phantom suitcase;
and that's me on a chilly street
15   walking at you, as if from a screen,
and blurring into blindness.

Oh . . . I sense inside my legs, grown heavy,
the trains that leave without me
and what a wealth of countries have not warmed me,
20   where I shan't live, and never shall be warmed!

And, in his armchair, the voyager from Eden
describes, his hands behind his head,
sucking the pipe smoke with a whistle,
his love of loves – a tropic bay.

The University Poem

1

'So then you're Russian? It's the first time
I have met a Russian . . .'
And the lively, delicately bulging
eyes examine me. 'You take your tea
with lemon, I already know.   5
I also know that you have icons
where you live, and samovars.'
A pretty girl. A British glow
spreads across her tender skin.
She laughs, she speaks at a quick clip: 10
'Frankly, our town is dullish,
though the river's charming!
Do you row?' Big girl,
with sloping shoulders, hands that are large,
bereft of rings.   15

2

Thus, at the vicar's, over tea,
brand-new acquaintances, we chat,
and I endeavor to be droll.
In troubling, dulcet worry lost
at the legs that she has crossed   5
and at her vivid lips I peer,
then, once again, I quickly shift
my cheeky gaze. She, as expected,
has come with aunt, although the latter
is busy with her left-wing patter – ,   10
and, contradicting her, the vicar,
a timid man (large Adam's apple),
with a brown-eyed, canine squint,
chokes upon a nervous cough.

3

Tea stronger than a Munich beer.
In the room the air is hazy.
In the hearth a flamelet lazy
gleams, like a butterfly on boulders.
I've overstayed – it's time to go now . . .
I rise; a nod, and then another,
I say good-bye without hand-thrusting,
For so demands the local custom;
I hurry down a step, and out
into a February day.
Out of the heavens, without a lull,
descends a ceaseless, two-week flow.
Isn't it true how very dull
an ancient student town can grow?

4

The houses – each more comely
than the next – whose ancient rosiness
gains cheer from bicycles reposing
near; the college gates by which
the bishop stands stonily inside his niche,
and higher, there is a black sun-like dial;
the fountains, hollow-sounding coolness,
the passageways, and then the barriers,
all iron roses with their thorns,
which, in the dark of early morn,
it is no easy task to climb;
and, right there, next door,
a tavern and an antique shop,
and beside a graveyard's tombstones
a thriving market in the square.

5

There is meat in hunks all pink;
the shiny fishes' uncooked stink;
and knives and pots; and also jackets

from wardrobes that shall remain nameless;
and, separate, in strange positions,   5
some crooked stands where they sold books
freeze motionless, as if concealing
some arcane alchemistic treatise;
one time I happened through this rubbish
to rummage, on a winter day,   10
when, adding to an exile's sadness,
it snowed, as in a Russian town –
I found some works by Pushkin, and
some Dahl upon a magic counter.

6

Behind this square's uneven outlines
there is a cinema, and thither
into the foggy depths we wandered,
where steeds midst swirls of dust rushed past
across the canvas screen of light,   5
the viewer magically alarming,
where, with a kiss's silhouette,
all ended at the proper time;
where tragedy was always sprinkled
with a beneficial lesson;   10
where droll and touching Charlie Chaplin
came mincing with his toes thrust out,
where, now and then, we chanced to yawn.

7

And, once again, the crooked alleys,
the gigantic age-old gates –
right in the center of the town,
a barber shop where they shaved Newton,
in ancient mystery enveloped,   5
the tavern known as the Blue Bull.
There, beyond the stream, the houses,
the century-old turf tramped down
into a dark-green, even carpet

to suit the needs of human games,
the wood-like sound of soccer kicks
in the cold air. Such was the world
where I from Russian clouds was hurled.

8

In the morning, out of bed I'd hop,
and to a lecture rush
with whistling cape; at last a hush
over the chilly amphitheater fell
as the professor of anatomy
mounted the podium, a sage
with vacant, childlike eyes;
with varicolored chalk
a Japanese design he'd trace
of intertwined blood vessels, or
the human skull, and on the way
a naughty joke he might let fly –
stamping of feet was our reply.

9

Supper. The regal dining hall
graced by the likeness of Henry the Eighth –
those tight-sheathed calves, that beard –
all by the sumptuous Holbein limned;
inside that singularly towering hall
that choir lofts made appear so tall,
it was perpetually murky
despite the violet conflagration,
that filtered through the colored panes.
The naked benches stretched along
the naked tables; there we sat,
in the black cowls of brothers' capes,
and ate the over-seasoned soups
made out of pallid vegetables.

10

I lived within an antique chamber,
but, inside its desert silence,
I hardly savored the shades' presence.
Clutching his bear from Muscovy,
esteemed the boxer's fate,   5
of Italic beauty dreaming
lame Byron passed his student days.
I remembered his distress –
his swim across the Hellespont
to lose some weight.   10
But I have cooled toward his creations . . .
so do forgive my unromantic side –
to me the marble roses of a Keats
have more charm than all those stagey storms.

11

But to think of poetry was harmful
in those years. To twist a screw of brass,
so that, in the water's droplets,
the world would radiantly appear
minute – that is what occupied my day.   5
I'm fond of the serene alignment
of green laboratory lamps,
the motley of the complex tables,
the magic gleam of instruments.
And from descending all day long   10
into the microscope's dark well
you did not hinder me at all.
O languorous Calliope,
the bane of uncompleted verse.

12

Instead, there was a new distraction:
something in my memory flashing,
as if unfocussed, and then clearer,
only to vanish once again.
Then I became abruptly bored   5
by work with needle and with screw,

33

observing the shimmer in the pattern,
of monotonous infusoria,
unraveling the bowels of a grass snake.
No longer did the lab seem heaven;
I started to imagine how, at the vicar's,
she and I would meet once more.

13

There! Now it's in focus. Now I see clearly.
It's there, the satiny-chestnut iridescent glimmer
of her coiffure, those somewhat crudely
penciled lips; those lips like bright-red wax
with minute fissures. Eyes half-closed
against the smoke, she finishes her cigarette
and, narrowing them, into the ashtray
the golden filter pokes . . . Soon the smoke will scatter,
her lashes will begin to flutter,
her sparkling eyes will glance intensely.
I'll be the first to lower my gaze.

14

Her name was not very becoming
(especially the British 'Violet'
to us was not pronounceable).
Quite unlike the flower, her eyes
blazed to the point of ugliness,
and on everything, with joy, intensely,
her humid gaze would long stay fixed,
her pupils curiously dilated . . .
Her speech, however, light and rapid,
was not consistent with her gaze,
and I myself could not decide
which I should trust – the vacuous chatter
or the grandiloquence of those eyes . . .

15

I knew, though, that her fullest blossom
Violet had achieved that year,
for how could she, a British girl,

34

enjoy her new-found liberty?
But three scant years remained
and she'd be thirty, all of thirty . . .
All those routine infatuations
And all had come and gone like shadows –
Jim, the soccer star, had vanished,
And Joe, the pensive one, and John,
of calculus the gloomy hero . . .
She flirted and procrastinated,
toyed superficially with love,
but in her heart awaited more.

16

Inevitably comes the day;
He's leaving, the ethereal friend:
the bill is paid, exams are done with,
the tennis racket in its frame,
and now the shiny locks click shut
on the suitcase filled to bursting.
He's leaving. From the anteroom
the luggage is brought out.
Some final clatter and the car moves off.
She gazes out into the dust:
oh, well – so be it. Once again
the phantom of the bridal veil
had in her dreams appeared in vain . . .
An empty alley, and, far off,
The grinding of the shifting gears . . .

17

From despicable influenza,
her father, a respected judge,
on Port an expert, and a joker,
had died not long ago, and
Violet resided with her aunt.
This lady was of the kind
of learned booby that abounds in England –
unlike her brother, thin and haughty,

she always used a walking stick,
she delivered lectures to the workers,
she revered culture's ideal
and considered – *inter al*. –
Kharkov a Russian general.

18

With her, Violet did not argue –
at times she might, but felt lethargic –
she lived in beneficial quiet,
she was ill versed in worldly matters,
recalling ever less her father,
her mother she'd forget (while I
by albums was informed about her –
about the times of wasp-waist dresses,
of horizontal boater hats.
The final snapshot: on a bench
she sat, and, down her lengthy skirt,
the shadows flowed onto the sand,
her necklet modest, pure her gaze,
a croquet mallet in her hand).

19

I was invited twice or thrice
to their hospitable house,
and at the theatre quite by chance,
Violet turned up next to me
(the students were performing *Hamlet*
and heaven was out of joint for
the bard's illustrious shade).
More often we would meet
in the vociferous evening street
when the horde of vendors seethes,
gutturally the news intoning.
That's the hour when she would walk.
Two words, a superficial joke,
the splendor of those somber eyes.

20

And then, one time – I recall clearly –,
in early March, in rainy weather,
it happened that the two of us
went to a soccer game together.
And, gradually, the crowd increased;   5
someone would crush my foot
or shove my shoulder; ever tighter
grew the many-headed roiling.
I entered into an unspoken resolution;
as soon as one goal shook the stands,   10
I would caress my Violet's hand.
Meanwhile in athletic shorts,
and in their motley jerseys clad,
the opposing players advanced.

21

Your average fan: under his cap
a squeamish lip and a strong whiff
of Virginia smoke. But now,
his lips unclench, his pipe's withdrawn;
another minute, mouth's agape;   5
another and he is howling. Hands
by the hundreds victory inciting:
an artful player propels the ball,
darts like a swallow the field's full length,
two men rush him, he swerves, he breaks through –   10
neat piece of work – and, on the run,
nets the tanned ball from afar
with a shot from his well-practiced toe.

22

I cautiously my hand extended
with faith in my internal pounding
that was repeating to me, 'touch . . .'
I touched. I was preparing even
to lean across, to whisper . . . She, though,   5
her tepid, unresponsive hand
disengaged without a word;

only then rang out her mirthful,
habitual voice, her merry laugh:
'Look – he plays worse than all the rest,
keeps falling all the time, poor chap . . .'
It was drizzling just a bit;
we were returning by the gully
where the black foliage decayed.

23

Home. Its pediments adorned
by coats of arms, the massive hall,
green glimpses of internal courts.
Silence reigned there. There, in the somber
dining hall (described above)
dwelt a staff of wizened waiters.
A sharp-eyed porter watched the gates.
There existed for the cleaning
of the obscure student lairs,
ever since immemorial times,
a diminutive breed of crones;
one of them would call on me
to brush the dust atop the dresser
and the shelves upon the wall.

24

And to forsake this final image
is hard for me. My memory
conserves her mouselike little steps,
her comical, funereal cap –
such as the one that was, perhaps,
worn by her grandma – the fine hairs
along her chin . . . Each morning, early,
amid the yellow-tinted fog,
without a sound, all dressed in black,
she would arrive, bringing the kindling,
and, like a rag doll, stoop in front
of the gelid morning hearth.
She'll spread the coke with practiced hand,
and, from below, scratch up a flame.

25

And this image is so troubling,
so bothersome to me . . . Perhaps,
in her dad's tobacco shop,
back in Queen Victoria's day,
her rosy girlishness had troubled   5
the hearts enclosed in checkered waistcoats –
the hearts of lanky students . . .
When there resounds in darkened elms,
the nightingale's sweet sound,
she would encounter one like me,   10
who with this spirited young girl
would snap the Persian lilac branches;
and to her bared and tilted neck
his impassioned lips would press.

26

Imagination rushes onward:
night, bedside table, lamp . . . sleep comes not
to the sick old man . . . immobile,
he hearkens to the nighttime whisper:
an experiment of vital import   5
has started in the lab . . . no strength left . . .
She comes when classes are to start,
She gathers up last midnight's clutter –
burnt cigarettes, a rusted pen nib;
she'll bring a pail out from the bedroom.   10
The professor's old. The time approaches
when he will die; he's long forgotten
the fragrance of tobaccos that
he smoked in Queen Victoria's days.

27

She's gone. Soundlessly the door has closed . . .
the blazing coals. Evening. Ennui . . .
and, deafened by the silence, I,
with my cake in raisins' birthmarks,
drink tea with gloomy *far niente*.   5
In the hearth, all tame and tender,

the fire's erect on its hind paws,
and the heat's rough-textured odor
of faded furniture is more intense
within my ancient little room.
To dig out with the red hot poker
concavities in hissing walls,
to play a solitary game of checkers,
to read, to write – what should I do?

28

Setting aside the dock-tailed teapot,
I take my faithful dictionary –
and with my muse, that wilted lady,
read in oppressive lassitude,
and locate in the final volume,
between 'free-loader' and 'hypocrite',
'despondence: melancholy, dejection, ennui;
spleen, hypochondria'.
and yet I will compose my poem . . .
Thus, for an hour or two, facing the fire,
I sit, I fit together rhymes,
having forgotten Violet –
and lo, like music from the heavens,
there peals the modulation of evening bells.

29

With opened window, to the bells
I hearken: for the night, the earth
is crossed by sacred quarter-notes,
on the far tower the hours resound,
the tower keeps count and then, more mournful,
another from afar responds.
Upon the buildings growing weighty,
the mantle of silence casts its folds. I hearken –
all has grown still. And my soul
to the stillness grows accustomed –
when suddenly, with thunderous guffaw,
swells up a motorcycle's gale
along the lifeless alleyways!

30

Since then my soul has lived more amply:
I understood in those years but a sampling
of earthly noises to the Lord is equal;
in that townlet in the towers' shadow
the sound of life was reckless clatter,
the mixture of tipsy antiquity
and of the present liveliness
were healthful for me: my soul's ready
to relish everything beneath the moon,
the ancient and the new.
But I am in disaccord with the moon's glow,
I try to avoid melancholy . . .
Oh keep me, Lord, from being a poet,
the earthly foolishly to miss!

31

No! I, with book and sleepy armchair
before a fireplace aglow,
did not let by, in useless sadness,
the charming entrance of the springtime.
I've had enough of coals and logs
stuck in the fireplace – till October.
Now the heavens are opened wide,
here, now, is the first lustrous crocus
that, like a mushroom, pierces grass,
and tomorrow, without copious tears,
without a lusty refrain,
she'll come and make herself at home –
a perfectly well-mannered girl,
quite unlike the Russian spring.

32

And now it's here. More limpid, higher
the chimes resound, and in his niche
the stony bishop leases out apartments
to the swallows. The hollow
honking in the alley's arch resounds
as sundry vehicles scuttle to and fro.

The fountain chirps, the barrier blooms.
Lawn tennis – that white pastime – replaces
boisterous soccer: in flannel trousers, the whole world
is off to play. Just then, the final
course was ending – the ultimate impasse,
and with Violet I would meet
and my Violet I would kiss.

33

Like the first time, she shied away
in my embrace – seemed horrified,
propped arms against my shoulders,
and how insane and mournful
looked her eyes! And this was neither
in amazement nor in anger,
nor was it stylized girlish fright . . .
I failed to understand . . . I do
recall the evenly and modishly
shorn garden, six white balls,
a row of massive rhododendron bushes;
a fiery player, I recollect
a court of firm-packed greensward, lined
with white and traversed by a net.

34

Her game was lazy – therefore, bad –
she played; she did not fly, chamois-like,
with the fleet foot of Lenglen.
Oh, I confess, my friends, I love
the stroke resilient at full tilt,
the goddess in a knee-length dress!
To toss the ball, to arch my back,
unwind like lightning,
with the stringed surface, from the shoulder
to skim the ball's occiput,
and, lunging, the whistling return
to devastatingly cut short –
the world has not a sweeter pastime . . .
in heaven we shall be playing ball.

35

A house of bricks stood by the stream:
ivy and the usual wisteria
entwined the wall betwixt the windows.
But, other than the plushy parlor,
where I remember three tableaux –   5
one of Mary by the Cross,
another, a huntsman in a red frock coat,
the third a group of sleeping dogs –
I saw none of the other rooms.
The fireplace, the bronze candlestick,   10
I guess I should also mention,
the pianola, too, beneath its cover,
and inadvertent feet that meshed
under the dainty teatime table.

36

She grew submissive very quickly . . .
For my part, I felt no reproach
in her obedience. The spring
changed imperceptibly to summer.
Through fields with Violet I amble: 5
sometimes the depths of a black cloud
would be encrimsoned by a sunset –
for Russia I so strongly yearned,
a nauseating heat would scald my soul,
especially when a mosquito   10
would whine above my ear in silent
evening hours, and my chest aches
from the aroma of bird cherry.
Enough, I will return one day.

37

Upon such days, with such-like sloth
who wants to study? And yet, alas,
exams impend, like it or not.
I guess we'll have to work a little . . .

The book, however, seems stale bread,
it's dry, it's stiff, I can't bite through.
We've overcome much more than that . . .
And now I spin in bacchanalias
of terms and systems' orgies,
and I remember midst all that
what a boat my friendly boatman
had promised me the previous day –
and all the unfinished volumes
slam shut and on their shelf. It's time!

38

Toward the festive, teeming river,
here and there the emerald sliver
of a geometric lawn descends,
or overhead an archway bends:
the waterway beneath is narrow
darkness, mold: into the turbid water
from both sides the Gothic walls ingrown.
Like otherworldly gobelins
the chestnuts bloom above the bridge,
and ivy on the centuries-old stone
crowds its ace-of-spades designs
and, further, like a narrow stripe,
the river winds past walls and towers
with a Venetian idleness.

39

There were the floats, pirogues, canoes;
yonder a gramophone, nearby
a vivid parasol, and petals
into the green-tinted water falling.
Love, drowsiness, the human crowd,
and through the antiquated bridges,
traversing the coolness of their ovals,
like some dream, both glossy and fatigued,
all of this slowly trickles past,

and iridesces, till, abducted   10
by a recondite meander
into a dense backwater of bird cherry
without reflection, without sound,
two beings 'neath an alder float.

40

Some wine, cold cutlets and some cushions,
Violet's patter, her softly breathing languorous breast,
encircled by a silken shawl;
her face, untouched by rouge,
was flaming. The pink chestnut tree   5
bloomed high above the alder forest.
The breeze was playing with the rushes,
rummaged through the boat, barely ruffled
a humorous review;
then on her palpitating neck   10
and the dimple of her clavicle
I kissed her, laughing.
I look: upon the colorful cushion
she pensively reclines.

41

She turns a page of the review,
and seemingly her gaze has stopped.
But that gaze was wearisome and dusky:
She did not see the printed page . . .
Abruptly, from beneath a throbbing eyelash,   5
emerged as from a chrysalis a bright ray
and down her ruddy-swarthy cheek,
glistening, a round diamond rolled . . .
'What is it, what,
please tell me?' Her shoulder   10
shrugged and heedlessly she wiped
the gleaming of that speechless tear,
with soundless laughter her throat swelled:
'I myself don't know, my dear one . . .'

42

The time ticked on. The sunset fog
descended. Far in the distance, indistinctly
in a pasture a horn sang. The world assumed
a crepuscular and misty cast. And in the colored lamellate
    small lantern
5   I light a candle, and quietly we sail
into the mist – was it not you,
Ophelia, or was it just the needle of a gramophone?
Within the mist an indefinable sound draws ever closer,
And, splashing a bit,
10 the shadow of a boat moves past,
a droplet of the flame glows red.

43

And perhaps it is not Violet –
But another, and in a different summer,
who on another night floats by my side . . .
you're here, and there was no parting,
5   you're here, and with extended hands
in the vague nocturnal silence,
you are in love with me again,
with you, amid the mirage riparian,
my happiness at last I've reached,
10 thank heaven, though, that very instant,
the rush of forbidden reverie
the sound of British speech cuts off:
'There's the landing, sweetheart, careful.'
I backed the oars and touched the shore.

44

There on the bench we sat a while . . .
'Oh, my Violet, don't tell me
that it's bedtime for you?'
And sparkling with her enlarged eyes,
5   she answers me: 'Judge for yourself, –
it's eleven o'clock,' – and, rising,

she offers me a last embrace.
And she adjusts her hairdo.
'I'll walk the final bit alone.
So long.' She's chilly once again,   10
and baleful, upset by something, –
hard to make out . . . I'm happy, though . . .
Lightly I am wafted by
the rapture of nocturnal being.

45

Homeward I walked, inebriated
in the tight embrace of charming alleys –
and my soul was so chock-full
and such a paucity of words!
Around – a dearth of sounds, of beings,   5
and, one would presume, a moon,
and spots of light on the smooth pavement,
that with my rubber heel I'd squash –
I walked and sang 'Alla verdy',
not sensing my approaching doom . . .   10
Ominously, gloomily,
from underneath an unseen gate,
suddenly there loomed the figures
of three most unseemly chaps.

46

Their chieftain – our most dogged mentor:
deportment, cape and the black
square (kerchief) covering his head –
his whole mien – severe reproach.
Two toughs – his faithful bulldogs –   5
stood flanking him and watching me.
They resembled two detectives,
but also two torch-bearing linkmen:
stocky, jowly, dressed in tailcoats
and top hats. And in the dim light   10
their quarry turned to flight.
The dark would hardly mean salvation.
Such fierce endurance they conceal and speed.

47

I stealthily the fiend evaded . . .
Alas, I was attired for sport,
while nighttime dress demanded, here
(see such-and-such clause of the rules),
that caps be worn. Another minute
all three of them would close on me,
the middle one's gaze would meet my gaze,
he'd ask my name, then write it down, –
as he pronounced a civil 'thank you';
and tomorrow there would be a reprimand and fine.
I froze. A whitish light was falling
on their indifferent features.
They moved in closer . . . and here I took,
as they say, to my heels.

48

The moon . . . The chase . . . The mad nightmare . . .
I run, I shun in silence:
then, either a top-hatted phantom
lunges or darkness threatens with its cloak,
or something like a hand
in a black glove . . . miss me, miss me . . .
and all is overwhelmed by moonlight,
all is distorted . . .
with a hurried jump
I ended my inglorious flight,
crawled into my college courtyard,
where no gliding angel passes,
and no wily demon.

49

I've become winded . . . My heart's beating . . .
The night oppresses me, listlessly flowing . . .
Into the coolness of my sheets
I slip when it's already dawning,
and in my dream I see you, Violet,
I hear you ask, 'Throw the cloak on . . .

No, no, not that one – it's too narrow . . .'
I dream that we converse in Russian,
and, in the dream, it's the familiar
form that we speak in, and I dream   10
you've brought some wood chips . . .
You break them, put them in the hearth . . .
Creep up, creep up, reluctant flamelet,
or will you disappear in smoke?

50

I got up late, slept through my classes . . .
The little crone cleaned my clothes –
the buttons knocked beneath her brush.
I dressed, and had a little smoke,
yawned to the Unicorn for lunch.   5
And suddenly there's Johnson at the door!
We had not met for half a year –
since he had taken his exam –
'Hello! I never thought I'd see you.'
'It's not for long, on Saturday I'm off,   10
I only need to grab some junk –
my last assignments to submit
where the local sages sit.'

51

We took a table. Appetizers,
small talk – a Russian's craving for caviar,
followed by the trout's blue curve, and talk
about who was now tennis champ,
then a rather silly argument   5
about the strike, and an airy cake.
Whereupon, having finished off
a bottle of amiable Graves,
then on the seductive Asti
we assiduously went to work –   10
about the emptiness of heart-throbs
vacuous discussions followed.

52

'– Love . . .' – and he gave a prolonged sigh:
'I loved once, too . . . Whom – it's no matter;
as soon as springtime dwindled,
I noticed that something was wrong;
my imagination cooled
and I lost my warmth toward her.'
He gave my glass a mournful clink
then he went on: 'It was awful . . .
you lean close to her, for instance,
and your wandering eye like Gulliver's
will see the giant furrows and the bumps
on what was once attractive to you,
and what you find repulsive since.'

53

Then he fell silent. We went out
together from the club. To be sincere,
I was a little high,
and felt like going home. The sun was hot.
Trees sparkled. Silently we paced,
When suddenly my gloomy partner –
on Holy Ghost Street –
squeezing my elbow, dryly uttered:
'I was just telling you . . . and look,
as chance would have it, here she is . . .'
and there was Violet, coming toward us,
gorgeous, happy, in a stream of sunlight.
She smiled at us, and off she went.

54

With a strange sense of irritation,
no longer tipsy, salutations
were exchanged with my chance partner,
I squandered a few hours, and – *basta* –
went to work – as I had seldom
worked, whole days, with bristling hair, I'd sink

into my studies, and not think
of leaving Violet, till, at last
(just like an oarsman straining with
approaching finish line in sight),   10
I crammed with textbooks through the night,
with ice against my brow pressed tight.

55

And it began. Exams went on
for five hot days. The torrid
sun so oppressively heated the hall
that someone fainted, and my neighbor
on the right a fit of sleeping sickness feigned   5
to conceal a failing mark.
And so it ended. Alma Mater
bestowed on each survivor's
brow a parting peck;
I gathered books and microscope, –   10
and suddenly I thought of Violet,
and that was when I thought with wonder
how the mysterious sequence
of centuries divided us.

56

And I, a liberated idler now,
with my free and hungry soul
went soaring off to other shores,
to a familiar port, where in an office
the indifferent sea recruits   5
simple hoboes such as me.
I have already squandered all my riches:
the well-known abbey's portrait
in two copies is all I have left.
And on the final night,   10
upon our lawn, amid
a Venetian court's habitual ball,
we undulated until dawn.

57

A gallery surrounds the court.
In the blue murk blushing pink,
garlands of lanterns glow –
Aeolus's airy swings.
Now the musicians join the fray,
five furiously moving shades
in a crimson shell of light.
And yet, amid all this, where's Violet?
I see her suddenly, standing
illumined by a lantern's glow,
between two columns, as on a stage,
something was drawing to a close . . .
Perhaps this dress with its black spangles
was not becoming to her?

58

Unperturbed by contact with her,
I cling to her as we start dancing;
she's silent and severe of bearing,
her immobile face asparkle.
And her resilient leg responds
to the pressure of my leg.
Obedient to the banging and the wailing,
the couples tread upon the lawn,
serpentines from every side,
and then the sax carries the tune,
now the drumsticks, then the rattles,
the exclamations of the cymbals,
first a long step, then a short one,
and night marvels at the ball.

59

A living soul yields not to fashion,
but, now and then, for freedom, passion
will coincide with its dictates . . .
I like the fox trot, forthright, gentle . . .
Some philosophizer, surely,

will find in it our epoch's symptoms,
debauchery to bedlam's music;
some literary lady or
dime-a-dozen poetaster
will bemoan the dances of the past;   10
but for my part, I'll say frankly,
I find no special charm at the sight of a boorish and
         unwashed
marquess dancing a minuet.

60

The band dies down. Beneath a colonnade
we walk . . .
Between one swallow and another
of lemonade she pattered then we sat down on the steps.
I look and see our comic shadows.   5
Our shadows touch: 'I'm off tomorrow, Violet.'
And uttering this was so simple . . .
Raising an eyebrow, she smiled at me . . .
a limpid smile: 'After a ball
it's easy to oversleep all trains.'   10
And the music moaned anew,
and we were dancing once again.

61

Oh cease, oh cease, my farewell ball!
While the festive wind lets drop
the colored ribbons on the sward and orange peels –
somewhere in her den
my little crone must be asleep – her sleep is peaceful.   5
Dapples of moonlight cling to her, her
dress lies like a black smudge on the chair,
her cap is like a black smudge on its hook;
the alarm clock with a sparkle 'neath its dome
assiduously ticks; under the cupboard a mouse   10
shuffles, darts away, and, in the stillness,
midst a serene snoring the pauper's night expires.

53

62

My little crone, at midday exactly,
will see me off. Lovingly, I screwed my racket
into its frame, knelt on my suitcase, snapped it shut.
Along the corners and the walls I let my soul and my gaze
      roam:
5   Yes, it's all packed . . . Farewell, my lair!
My little crone is at the door . . .
The thunderous motor's rumble – the wheels move off . . .
Oh well, another one is gone . . . A fresh one
will move in, come October – and the talk
10   will be the same, with the same rubbish on the rug . . .

63

And that is all. Farewell, dear sounds,
farewell, fair muse.
Before our parting I ask only one thing:
as you fly, swallowlike, now lower,
5   now on high, find one plain word within this world,
always swift to understand you,
where moth and rust do not corrupt,
cherishing each instant,
blessing each motion,
10   do not allow it to freeze still,
perceive the delicate rotation
of the slightly tilted earth.

Butterflies

... From afar you can discern the swallowtail
from its sunny, tropic beauty:
along a grassy slope it dashes
and settles on a roadside dandelion.
My net swings, the muslin loudly rustles.   5
O, yellow demon, how you quiver!
I am afraid to tear its dentate little fringes
and its black, supremely slender tails.
Also, on occasion in the oriole-filled park,
some lucky midday, hot and windy,   10
I'd stand, ecstatic at the fragrance,
before a tall and fluffy lilac,
almost crimson in comparison
with the deep blue of the sky,
and, dangling from a cluster, palpitating,   15
the swallowtail, a gold-winged guest, grew tipsy,
while, blindingly, the wind was swaying
both butterfly and luscious cluster.
You aim, but the branches interfere;
you swing – but with a flash it vanishes,   20
and from the net turned inside out
tumble only severed crests of flowers.

Tolstoy

A picture in a school anthology:
an old man, barefoot. As I turned the page,
unkindled still was my imagination.
With Pushkin things are different: there's the cloak,
the cliff, the foaming surf . . . The surname 'Pushkin'
grows over, ivylike, with poetry,
and repetitiously the muse cites names
that echo noisily around him: Delvig,
Danzas, d'Anthès – and his whole life has a
romantic ring, from school-day Delia to
the pistol shot, that chill day of the duel.
The radiance of legend has as yet
not touched Tolstoy. His life does not arouse
a feeling of excitement. Names of people
connected with him still do not sound ripe:
with time they'll gain mysterious distinction;
that time has not yet come: my naming Chertkov
would just mean narrowing the poem's horizon.
One should say, too, that people's memory
must lose material contact with the past
in order to make gossip into epic
and to transmute the muteness into music,
while we are still unable to renounce
too-flattering proximity to him
in time. It's likely our grandchildren will
regard us with unreasonable envy.
Insidious technology sometimes
can bolster memory artificially.
A phonograph recording still preserves
the cadence of his voice: he reads aloud,
monotonously, hastily, opaquely,
and stumbling when he comes to the word 'God',

repeating 'God', and then continuing –
a slightly husky, almost senseless sound,
like someone coughing in the next compartment   35
when, in the old days, at a nighttime station,
your railroad car would make a sighing stop.
In an archive of ancient films, they say
(which blink, these days, as though with dimming vision)
there is a Yasnaya Polyana sequence;   40
a nondescript old man of modest stature,
his beard disheveled by the wind, who walks
by with accelerated little steps,
disgruntled by the cameraman. And we're
content. He's close and comprehensible.   45
We've visited with him, we've sat together.
There's nothing awesome in this genius speaking
of matrimony or of peasant schools . . .
And, with a feeling that he is our equal,
with whom it is all right to argue some,   50
addressing him by name and patronymic,
we smile with deference and discuss together
his views on this or that . . . The windbags buzz
around the evening samovar; upon
a spotless tablecloth flit shadows of   55
religions, of philosophies, of states –
the humble soul's delight . . .
                              Yet there remains
one thing we simply cannot reconstruct,
no matter how we poke, armed with our notepads,
just like reporters at a fire, around   60
his soul. It's to a certain secret throbbing –
the essence – that our access is denied.
The mystery is almost superhuman!
I mean the nights on which Tolstoy composed;
I mean the miracle, the hurricane   65
of images flying across the inky
expanse of sky in that hour of creation,
that hour of incarnation . . . For, the people
born on those nights were real . . . That's how the Lord

57

70 transmits to his elected his primeval,
    his beatific license to create
    his worlds, and instantly to breathe into
    the new-made flesh a one-and-only spirit.
    And here they are, alive; all, in them, lives –
75 their habits, their locutions, and their mores:
    their homeland is that special kind of Russia
    we carry in the depths where there exists
    a blurry dream of signs ineffable:
    a Russia of smells, of nuances, of sounds,
80 of giant clouds above at haying time,
    a Russia of fascinating swamplands, where
    wild game abounds . . . Those are the things we love.
    The people he created, thousands of them,
    transpire incredibly through our own life,
85 lend color to the distance of recall –
    as though we actually lived beside them.
    On various occasions, midst the crowd,
    to note Karenina's black curls we've chanced,
    and with little Shcherbatskaya we've danced
90 her vainly saved mazurka at the ball . . .
    I feel that rhymes, like blooms, within me stir:
    the wing's invisible, I heed its call . . .
    I know that death is just a kind of border;
    yet I see death as a specific image:
95 the final page's text is now in order,
    the lamp extinguished o'er the desk. The vision
    keeps shimmering, prolonged by its reflection,
    then, suddenly, unthinkably, it ends . . .
    And he is gone, meticulous creator
100 who into lucid voices separated
    the din of being, a din he understood . . .
    One day, from a chance railroad station, he
    turned off toward the unknown and left for good;
    beyond lies night, silence, and mystery . . .

I have no need, for my nocturnal travels,
    of ships, I have no need of trains.
The moon's above the checkerboard-like garden.
    The window's open. I am set.

And with habitual silence – like a tomcat,   5
    at night over a fence – across
the border streamlet, passportless, my shadow
    leaps to the other, Russian, bank.

Mysterious, invulnerable, weightless,
    I glide across successive walls,   10
and at the moonlight, the dream rushing past him,
    the border guard takes aim in vain.

I fly across the meadows, dance through forests –
    and who will know that there exists
in this vast country but a single living,   15
    a single happy citizen.

Along the lengthy quay the Neva shimmers.
    All's still. A tardy passer-by
my shadow in a lonely square encounters
    and curses his own fantasy.   20

Now I approach an unfamiliar building,
    the place alone I recognize . . .
There, in the darkened rooms, everything's altered,
    and everything upsets my shade.

There, children sleep. Above the pillow's corner
  I stoop, and they begin to dream
about the toys that, long ago, I played with,
  about my ships, about my trains.

To the Grapefruit

Resplendent fruit, so weighty and so glossy,
exactly like a full-blown moon you shine;
hermetic vessel of unsweet ambrosia
and aromatic coolness of white wine.

The lemon is the pride of Syracuse,   5
Mignon yields to the orange's delights,
but you alone are fit to quench the Muse
when, thirsty, she has come down from her heights.

The Hawkmoth

Long and hazy the evening,
and I stand, as in prayer,
a young entomologist,
with some honeysuckle near.
How I crave, unexpected,
Midst those flowers to glimpse,
With proboscis projected,
a heavenly sphinx!
A quick throb – and I see it.
At an angel I hit,
and a demon's entangled
in the haze of my net.

Forty-three years, forty-four years maybe,
had elapsed since I recalled you last:
then, with neither reason nor transition,
there you were, dream caller from the past,

I, to whom is, nowadays, repugnant   5
every detail of that bygone life,
felt that some insinuating, willful
bawd had prearranged a tryst with you.

But, although the same guitar you fingered,
sang again 'I was a newlywed . . .'   10
you weren't here to rend me with old anguish,
only to announce that you were dead.

To Véra

To the steppes, they will drive them, O Harlequins mine,
through ravines, to the realms of strange hetmans!
Their geometry and their Venetian design
they will call but eccentric deception.

5   You alone, you alone, as they passed, were agog
at the black, blue, and orange-hued rhombi . . .
'An unusual writer, N. – athlete and snob,
and endowed with enormous aplomb, he . . .'

The Russian Poems from
Poems and Problems

The Rain Has Flown

The rain has flown and burnt up in flight.
   I tread the red sand of a path.
Golden orioles whistle, the rowan is in bloom,
   the catkins on sallows are white.

The air is refreshing, humid and sweet.   5
   How good the caprifole smells!
Downward a leaf inclines its tip
   and drops from its tip a pearl.

To Liberty

Slowly you wander through the sleepless streets.
From your sad brow gone is the former ray,
that called us toward love and shining heights.
Your trembling hand holds an extinguished taper.
Dragging your broken wing over dead men,
your bloodstained elbow covering your eyes,
once more deceived, you once again depart,
and the old night, alas, remains behind.

I Still Keep Mute

I still keep mute – and in the hush grow strong.
The far-off crests of future works, amidst
the shadows of my soul are still concealed
like mountaintops in pre-auroral mist.

I greet you, my inevitable day!   5
The skyline's width, variety and light
increase; and on the first, resounding step
I go up, filled with terror and delight.

Hotel Room

Not quite a bed, not quite a bench.
Wallpaper: a grim yellow.
A pair of chairs. A squinty looking-glass.
We enter – my shadow and I.

We open with a vibrant sound the window:
the light's reflection slides down to the ground.
The night is breathless. Distant dogs
with varied barks fracture the stillness.

Stirless, I stand there at the window,
and in the black bowl of the sky
glows like a golden drop of honey
    the mellow moon.

Provence

I wander aimlessly from lane to lane,
bending a careful ear to ancient times:
the same cicadas sang in Caesar's reign,
upon the walls the same sun clings and climbs.

The plane tree sings: with light its trunk is pied;   5
the little shop sings: delicately tings
the bead-stringed curtain that you push aside –
and, pulling on his thread, the tailor sings.

And at a fountain with a rounded rim,
rinsing blue linen, sings a village girl,   10
and mottle shadows of the plane tree swim
over the stone, the wickerwork, and her.

What bliss it is, in this world full of song,
to brush against the chalk of walls, what bliss
to be a Russian poet lost among   15
cicadas trilling with a Latin lisp!

La Bonne Lorraine

The English burned her, burned my girl,
burned her in Rouen's market square.
The deathsman sold me a black coat of mail,
a beaked helmet and a dead spear.

You are here with me, iron saint,
and the world has grown cold and stark:
slanting shadows, and winding stairs,
and the night's velvet nailed with stars.

Above rusty traceries, my candle
flickers and drops wax on the straps.
We, warriors, flew in your wake
and tinctured our days in your colors.

But when night lowered its vizor,
in silence you slipped out of masculine armor,
and white and weak you would burn
in the embrace of your faithful knights.

The Blazon

As soon as my native land had receded
in the briny dark the northeaster struck,
like a sword of diamond revealing
among the clouds a chasm of stars.

My yearning ache, my recollections   5
I swear to preserve with royal care
ever since I adopted the blazon of exile:
on a field of sable a starry sword.

The Mother

Night falls. He has been executed.
From Golgotha the crowd descends and winds
between the olive trees, like a slow serpent;
and mothers watch as John downhill
5   into the mist, with urgent words, escorts
    gray, haggard Mary.

To bed he'll help her, and lie down himself,
and through his slumber hear till morning
    her tossings and her sobs.
10   What if her son had stayed at home with her,
and carpentered and sung? What if those tears
    cost more than our redemption?

The Son of God will rise, in radiance orbed;
on the third day a vision at the tomb
15   will meet the wives who bought the useless myrrh;
Thomas will feel the luminescent flesh;
the wind of miracles will drive men mad,
    and many will be crucified.

Mary, what are to you the fantasies
20   of fishermen? Over your grief days skim
    insensibly, and neither on the third
nor hundredth, never will he heed your call
and rise, your brown firstborn who baked mud sparrows
    in the hot sun, at Nazareth.

I Like That Mountain

I like that mountain in its black pelisse
of fir forests – because
in the gloom of a strange mountain country
I am closer to home.

How should I not know those dense needles,   5
and how should I not lose my mind
at the mere sight of that peatbog berry
showing blue along my way?

The higher the dark and damp
trails twist upward, the clearer   10
grow the tokens, treasured since childhood,
of my northern plain.

Shall we not climb thus
the slopes of paradise, at the hour of death,
meeting all the loved things   15
that in life elevated us?

The Dream

To my alarm clock its lesson I set
for next morning, and into the darkness
I release my bedroom like a balloon,
and step into sleep with relief.

5   Then, in sleep itself, I'm possessed by a sort
of subordinate drowsiness. Dimly
I see a round table. I cannot make out
those sitting at it. We're all waiting for somebody.

One of the guests has a pocket flashlight
10   that he trains on the door, like a pistol;
and higher in stature, and brighter in face
a dead friend of mine enters, laughing.

Without any astonishment I talk to him,
now alive, and I feel there is no deception.
15   The once mortal wound has gone from his brow
as if it had been some light make-up.

We talk, I feel gay. Then, suddenly,
there's a falter, an odd embarrassment.
My friend leads me aside
20   and whispers something in explanation.

But I do not hear. A long-ringing bell
summons to the performance:
the alarm clock repeats its lesson
and daylight breaks through my eyelids.

Looking, just for one moment, of the wrong shape,   25
the world lands catlike, on all
its four feet at once, and now stands
familiar both to the mind and the eye.

But, good Lord – when by chance the dream is recalled
during the day, in somebody's drawing room,   30
or when in a flash it comes back to one
in front of a gunsmith's window –

how grateful one is to unearthly powers
that the dead can appear in one's sleep,
how proud of the dream, of that nighttime event,   35
is one's shaken soul!

The Snapshot

Upon the beach at violet-blue noon,
in a vacational Elysium
a striped bather took
a picture of his happy family.

And very still stood his small naked boy,
and his wife smiled,
in ardent light, in sandy bliss
plunged as in silver.

And by the striped man
directed at the sunny sand
blinked with a click of its black eyelid
the camera's ocellus.

That bit of film imprinted
all it could catch,
the stirless child,
his radiant mother,

and a toy pail and two beach spades,
and some way off a bank of sand,
and I, the accidental spy,
I in the background have been also taken.

Next winter, in an unknown house,
grandmother will be shown an album,
and in that album there will be a snapshot,
and in that snapshot I shall be.

My likeness among strangers,
one of my August days,
my shade they never noticed,
my shade they stole in vain.

In Paradise

My soul, beyond distant death
your image I see like this:
a provincial naturalist,
an eccentric lost in paradise.

5   There, in a glade, a wild angel slumbers,
a semi-pavonian creature.
Poke at it curiously
with your green umbrella,

speculating how, first of all,
10 you will write a paper on it,
then — — But there are no learned journals,
nor any readers in paradise!

And there you stand, not yet believing
your wordless woe.
15 About that blue somnolent animal
whom will you tell, whom?

Where is the world and the labeled roses,
the museum and the stuffed birds?
And you look and look through your tears
20 at those unnamable wings.

The Execution

On certain nights as soon as I lie down
my bed starts drifting into Russia,
and presently I'm led to a ravine,
to a ravine led to be killed.

I wake – and in the darkness, from a chair   5
where watch and matches lie,
into my eyes, like a gun's steadfast muzzle,
the glowing dial stares.

With both hands shielding breast and neck –
now any instant it will blast! –   10
I dare not turn my gaze away
from that disk of dull fire.

The watch's ticking comes in contact
with frozen consciousness;
the fortunate protection   15
of my exile I repossess.

But how you would have wished, my heart,
that *thus* it all had really been:
Russia, the stars, the night of execution
and full of racemosas the ravine!   20

For Happiness the Lover
Cannot Sleep

For happiness the lover cannot sleep;
the clock ticktacks; the gray-haired merchant fancies
in vermeil skies a silhouetted crane,
into a hold its cargo slowly sinking.
To gloomy exiles there appears miraged
a mist, which youth with its own hue has tinted.

Amidst the agitation and the beauty
of daily life, one image everywhere
haunts me incessantly, torments and claims me:

Upon the bright-lit island of the desk
the somber facets of the open inkstand
and the white sheet of paper, and the lamp's
unswitched-off light beneath its green glass dome.

And left athwart the still half-empty page,
my pen like a black arrow, and the word
I did not finish writing.

Lilith

I died. The sycamores and shutters
along the dusty street were teased
by torrid Aeolus.
                        I walked,
and fauns walked, and in every faun
god Pan I seemed to recognize: 5
Good. I must be in Paradise.

Shielding her face and to the sparkling sun
showing a russet armpit, in a doorway
there stood a naked little girl.
She had a water lily in her curls   10
and was as graceful as a woman. Tenderly
her nipples bloomed, and I recalled
the springtime of my life on earth,
when through the alders on the river brink
so very closely I could watch   15
the miller's youngest daughter as she stepped
out of the water, and she was all golden,
with a wet fleece between her legs.

And now, still wearing the same dress coat
that I had on when killed last night,   20
with a rake's predatory twinkle,
toward my Lilith I advanced.
She turned upon me a green eye
over her shoulder, and my clothes
were set on fire and in a trice   25
dispersed like ashes.
                        In the room behind
one glimpsed a shaggy Greek divan,

on a small table wine, pomegranates,
and some lewd frescoes covering the wall.
With two cold fingers childishly
she took me by my emberhead:
'now come along with me,' she said.

Without inducement, without effort,
Just with the slowness of pert glee,
like wings she gradually opened
her pretty knees in front of me.
And how enticing, and how merry,
her upturned face! And with a wild
lunge of my loins I penetrated
into an unforgotten child.
Snake within snake, vessel in vessel,
smooth-fitting part, I moved in her,
through the ascending itch forefeeling
unutterable pleasure stir.
But suddenly she lightly flinched,
retreated, drew her legs together,
and grasped a veil and twisted it
around herself up to the hips,
and full of strength, at half the distance
to rapture, I was left with nothing.
I hurtled forward. A strange wind
caused me to stagger. 'Let me in!'
I shouted, noticing with horror
that I again stood outside in the dust
and that obscenely bleating youngsters
were staring at my pommeled lust.
'Let me come in!' And the goat-hoofed,
copper-curled crowd increased. 'Oh, let me in,'
I pleaded, 'otherwise I shall go mad!'
The door stayed silent, and for all to see
writhing with agony I spilled my seed
and knew abruptly that I was in Hell.

The Muse

Your coming I recall: a growing vibrance,
an agitation to the world unknown.
The moon through branches touched the balcony
and there a shadow, lyriform, was thrown.

To me, a youth, the iamb seemed a garb   5
too rude for the soft languor of your shoulders;
but my imperfect line had tunefulness
and with the red lips of its rhyme it smiled.

And I was happy. On the dimming desk
a trembling flame hollowed my bit of candle,   10
and in my dream the page was under glass,
immortal, all zigzagged with my corrections.

Not so at present. For the morning star
my morning slumber I will not surrender.
Beyond my strength are multitudes of tasks –   15
especially the worries of ambition.

I am expert, frugal, intolerant.
My polished verse cleaner than copper shines.
We talk occasionally, you and I,
across the fence like two old country neighbors.   20

Yes, ripeness is pictorial, agreed:
leaf of grapevine, pear, watermelon halved,
and – top of artistry – transparent light.
I'm feeling cold. Ah, this is autumn, Muse!

Soft Sound

When in some coastal townlet, on a night
of low clouds and ennui, you open
the window – from afar
whispering sounds spill over.

Now listen closely and discern
the sound of seawaves breathing upon land,
protecting in the night
the soul that harkens unto them.

Daylong the murmur of the sea is muted,
but the unbidden day now passes
(tinkling as does an empty
tumbler on a glass shelf);

and once again amidst the sleepless hush
open your window, wider, wider,
and with the sea you are alone
in the enormous and calm world.

Not the sea's sound . . . In the still night
I hear a different reverberation:
the soft sound of my native land,
her respiration and pulsation.

Therein blend all the shades of voices
so dear, so quickly interrupted
and melodies of Pushkin's verse
and sighs of a remembered pine wood.

Repose and happiness are there,   25
a blessing upon exile;
yet the soft sound cannot be heard by day
drowned by the scurrying and rattling.

But in the compensating night,
in sleepless silence, one keeps listening   30
to one's own country, to her murmuring,
her deathless deep.

Snow

Oh, that sound! Across snow –
creak, creak, creak:
somebody walking in long boots of felt.

Stout, spirally twisted ice,
sharp points inverted, hangs from the eaves.
The snow is crumpy and shiny.
   (Oh, that sound!)

My hand sled behind me, far from dragging,
seems to run by itself: it knocks at my heels.

I settle upon it and coast
down the steep, down the smooth:
felt boots straddled,
I hold on to the string.

Whenever I'm falling asleep,
I cannot help think:
Maybe you will find a moment
   to visit me,
my warmly muffled up, clumsy
   childhood.

The Formula

Humped up on the back of a chair,
    a fingerless overcoat.
The darkening day was deceptive:
    fancy has it all wrong.

A current of air has passed recently   5
    and one's soul has been blown
into a flowingly opening
    cipher of glass.

Filtered through light as reflected
    by the vessels of numbers,   10
bloated or flattened
    in curved limbs of alembics,

my spirit was being transfigured
    into thousands of rings,
which gyrated and multiplied   15
    and at last it all came to a stop,

in most crystal stagnation,
    most excellent Nought;
and in my room just an empty
    overcoat hunches its back.

An Unfinished Draft

The poet dealing in Dejection
to Beauty iterates: adieu!
He says that human days are only
words on a page picked up by you
upon your way (a page ripped out –
where from? You know not and reject it)
or from the night into the night
through a bright hall a brief bird's flight.

Zoilus (a majestic rascal,
whom only lust of gain can stir)
and Publicus, litterateur
(a nervous leaseholder of glory),
cower before me in dismay
because I'm wicked, cold, and gay,
because honor and life I weigh
on Pushkin's scales and dare prefer
honor . . .

Evening on a Vacant Lot

In memory of V. D. N.

Inspiration, rosy sky,
black house, with a single window,
fiery. Oh, that sky
drunk up by the fiery window!
Trash of solitary outskirts,   5
weedy little stalk with teardrop,
skull of happiness, long, slender,
like the skull of a borzoi.
What's the matter with me? Self-lost,
melting in the air and sunset,   10
muttering and almost fainting
on the waste at eveningtime.
Never did I want so much to cry.
Here it is, deep down in me.
The desire to bring it forth intact,   15
slightly filmed with moisture and so tremulous,
never yet had been so strong in me.
Do come out, my precious being,
cling securely to a stem,
to the window, still celestial,   20
or to the first lighted lamp.
Maybe empty is the world, and brutal;
nothing do I know – except
that it's worthwhile being born
for the sake of this your breath.   25

It once was easier and simpler:
two rhymes – and my notebook I'd open.
How hazily I got to know you
in my presumptuous youth!
Leaning my elbows on the railing   30

of verse that glided like a bridge,
already I imagined that my soul
had started moving, started gliding,
and would keep drifting to the very stars.
But when transcribed in a fair copy,
deprived of magic instantly,
how helplessly behind each other
the leaden-weighted words would hide!

My young loneliness
in the night among motionless boughs!
The amazement of night over the river,
which reflects it in full;
and lilac bloom, the pale darling
of my first inexperienced numbers,
with that fabulous moonlight upon it!
And the paths of the park in half-mourning,
and – enlarged at present by memory,
twice as solid and beautiful now,
the old house, and the deathless flame
of the kerosene lamp in the window;
and in sleep the nearing of bliss,
a far breeze, an aerial envoy
with increasing noise penetrating dense woods,
inclining a branch at last –
all that time had seemed to have taken,
but you pause, and again it shines through,
for its lid was not tight – and no longer
can one take it away from you.

Blinking, a fiery eye looks,
through the fingerlike black stacks
of a factory, at weedy flowers
and a deformed tin can.
Across the vacant lot in darkening dust
I glimpse a slender hound with snow-white coat.
Lost, I presume. But in the distance sounds

insistently and tenderly a whistling.
And in the twilight toward me a man
comes, calls. I recognize
your energetic stride. You haven't
changed much since you died.   70

The Madman

A street photographer in laic life,
now poet, king, Parnassian autocrat
(since quite a time kept under lock and key),
thus did he speak:
                              I did not wish to stoop
5   to Fame: it rushed up of its own accord.
I've now forgotten where my Muse was schooled.
Straight, lonesome was her path. I never knew
how to stock friends for use, nor to pull thorns
from lion paws. It suddenly began
10   to snow; surprising! It was snowing roses.

Enchanting destiny! How much I prize
an Enemy's wan little smile! I like
to incommode the Failure, multiply
his painful dreams about me, and examine
15   the skeleton of Envy, shadowgraphed
and showing through, if held up to the light.

When I with balladry blandish the moon
the trees beyond the gate grow agitated
as they endeavor out of turn to get
20   into my verse. I'm privileged to rule
the entire world (which disobeys my Neighbor),
and happiness so airily dilates,
my head is filled with such an incandescence,
and words of such impeccable perfection
25   come to meet Thought and wing away with her
that I dare not write down a single word.

Yet sometimes – Oh to be another! Quick!
Another! Tailor, carpenter – Or, say,
itinerant photographer: to live
as in an old tale, work the villas, take   30
pictures of dappled children in a hammock,
and of their dog and shadows on the sand.

How I Love You

Kind of green, kind of gray, i.e.,
striated all over with rain,
and the linden fragrance, so heady,
that I can hardly—— Let's go!
Let's go and abandon this garden
and the rain that seethes on its paths
between the flowers grown heavy,
kissing the sticky loam.
Let's go, let's go before it's too late,
quick, under one cloak, come home,
while you still are unrecognized,
my mad one, my mad one!

Self-control, silence. But with each year,
to the murmur of trees and the clamor of birds,
the separation seems more offenseful
and the offense more absurd.
And I fear ever more that rashly
I may blab and interrupt
the course of the quiet, difficult speech
long since penetrating my life.

Above red-cheeked slaves
the blue sky looks all lacquered,
and pumped-up clouds
with scarcely discernible jerks
    move across.
I wonder, is there nowhere a place there,
to lie low – some dark nook
where the darkness might merge

with a wing's cryptic markings?
(A geometrid thus does not stir   30
spread flat on a lichened trunk.)

What a sunset! And once more tomorrow
and for a long time the heat is to last,
a forecast faultlessly based
on the stillness and on the gnats: 35
hanging up in an evening sunbeam,
their swarmlet ceaselessly jiggles,
reminding one of a golden toy
in the hands of a mute peddler.

How I love you! In this   40
evening air, now and then,
the spirit finds loopholes, translucences
in the world's finest texture.
The beams pass between tree trunks.

How I love you! The beams   45
pass between tree trunks; they band
the tree trunks with flame. Do not speak.
Stand motionless under the flowering branch,
inhale – what a spreading, what flowing! –
Close your eyes, and diminish, and stealthily   50
    into the eternal pass through.

L'Inconnue de la Seine

Urging on this life's denouement,
loving nothing upon this earth,
I keep staring at the white mask
of your lifeless face.

Strings, vibrating and endlessly dying,
with the voice of your beauty call.
Amidst pale crowds of drowned young maidens
you're the palest and sweetest of all.

In music at least linger with me!
Your lot was chary of bliss.
Oh, reply with a posthumous half-smile
of your charmed gypsum lips!

Immobile and convex the eyelids.
Thickly matted the lashes. Reply –
can this be for ever, for ever?
Ah, the way they could glance, those eyes!

Touchingly frail young shoulders,
the black cross of a woolen shawl,
the streetlights, the wind, the night clouds,
the harsh river dappled with dark.

Who was he, I beseech you, tell me,
your mysterious seducer? Was he
some neighbor's curly-locked nephew
of the loud tie and gold-capped tooth?

Or a client of star-dusted heavens,   25
friend of bottle, billiards, and dice,
the same sort of accursed man of pleasure
and bankrupt dreamer as I?

And right now, his whole body heaving,
he, like me, on the edge of his bed,   30
in a black world long empty, sits staring
    at a white mask?

At Sunset

At sunset, by the same bench,
as in the days of my youth,

At sunset, you know the kind,
with a bright-colored cloud and a chafer,

At the bench with the half-rotten board,
high above the incarnadine river,

As then, in those distant days,
smile and avert your face,

If to souls of those long dead
it is given sometimes to return.

We So Firmly Believed

We so firmly believed in the linkage of life,
but now I've looked back – and it is astonishing
to what a degree you, my youth,
seem in tints not mine, in traits not real.

If one probes it, it's rather like a wave's haze   5
between me and you, between shallow and sinking,
or else I see telegraph poles and you from the back
as right into the sunset you ride your half-racer.

You've long ceased to be I. You're an outline – the hero
of any first chapter; yet how long we believed   10
that there was no break in the way from the damp dell
   to the alpine heath.

What Happened Overnight

What happened overnight to memory?
It must have snowed: such stillness! Of no use
Was to my soul the study of Oblivion:
that problem has been solved in sleep.

A simple, elegant solution.
(Now what have I been bothering about
so many years?) One does not see much need
in getting up: there's neither bed, nor body.

The Poets

From room to hallway a candle passes
and is extinguished. Its imprint swims in one's eyes,
until, among the blue-black branches,
a starless night its contours finds.

It is time, we are going away: still youthful,   5
with a list of dreams not yet dreamt,
with the last, hardly visible radiance of Russia
on the phosphorent rhymes of our last verse.

And yet we did know – didn't we? – inspiration,
we would live, it seemed, and our books would grow,   10
but the kithless muses at last have destroyed us,
and it is time now for us to go.

And this not because we're afraid of offending
with our freedom good people; simply, it's time
for us to depart – and besides we prefer not   15
to see what lies hidden from other eyes;

not to see all this world's enchantment and torment,
the casement that catches a sunbeam afar,
humble somnambulists in soldier's uniform,
the lofty sky, the attentive clouds;   20

the beauty, the look of reproach; the young children
who play hide-and-seek inside and around
the latrine that revolves in the summer twilight;
the sunset's beauty, its look of reproach;

all that weighs upon one, entwines one, wounds one;
an electric sign's tears on the opposite bank;
through the mist the stream of its emeralds running;
all the things that already I cannot express.

In a moment we'll pass across the world's threshold
into a region – name it as you please:
wilderness, death, disavowal of language,
or maybe simpler: the silence of love;

the silence of a distant cartway, its furrow,
beneath the foam of flowers concealed;
my silent country (the love that is hopeless);
the silent sheet lightning, the silent seed.

To Russia

Will you leave me alone? I implore you!
Dusk is ghastly. Life's noises subside.
I am helpless. And I am dying
Of the blind touch of your whelming tide.

He who freely abandons his country   5
on the heights to bewail it is free.
But now I am down in the valley
and now do not come close to me.

I'm prepared to lie hidden forever
and to live without name. I'm prepared,   10
lest we only in dreams come together,
all conceivable dreams to forswear;

to be drained of my blood, to be crippled,
to have done with the books I most love,
for the first available idiom   15
to exchange all I have: my own tongue.

But for that, through the tears, oh, Russia,
through the grass of two far-parted tombs,
through the birchtree's tremulous macules,
through all that sustained me since youth,   20

with your blind eyes, your dear eyes, cease looking
at me, oh, pity my soul,
do not rummage around in the coalpit,
do not grope for my life in this hole

because years have gone by and centuries,
and for sufferings, sorrow, and shame,
too late – there is no one to pardon
and no one to carry the blame.

Oculus

To a single colossal oculus,
without lids, without face, without brow,
without halo of marginal flesh,
man is finally limited now.

And without any fear having glanced   5
at the earth (quite unlike the old freak
that was dappled all over with seas
and smiled with the sun on one cheek),

not mountains he sees and not waves,
not some gulf that brilliantly shines,   10
and not the silent old cinema
of clouds, and grainfields, and vines,

and of course not a part of the parlor
with his kin's leaden faces – oh, no,
in the stillness of his revolutions   15
nothing in that respect will he know.

Gone, in fact, is the break between matter
and eternity; and who can care
for a world of omnipotent vision,
if nothing is monogrammed there?   20

Fame

And now there rolls in, as on casters, a character,
waxlike, lean-loined, with red nostrils soot-stuffed,
and I sit and cannot decide: is it human
or nothing special – just garrulous dust?

5   Like a blustering beggar, the pest of the poorhouse,
like an evil old schoolmate, like the head spy
(in that thick slurred murmur: 'Say, what were you doing
in such and such place?'), like a dream,

like a spy, like a hangman, like an evil old schoolmate,
10 like the Influence on the Balkan Novella of – er –
the Symbolist School, only worse. There are matters, matters,
which, so to speak, even . . . (Akakiy Akakievich

had a weakness, if you remember, for 'weed words',
and he's like an Adverb, my waxy guest),
15 and my heart keeps pressing, and my heart keeps tossing,
and I can't any more – while his speech

fairly tumbles on downhill, like sharp loose gravel,
and the burry-R'd meek heart must harken to him,
aye, harken entranced to the buoyant gentleman
20 because it has got no words and no fame.

Like a mockery of conscience in a cheap drama,
like a hangman, and shiverings, and the last dawn –
Oh, wave, swell up higher! The stillness is grateful
for the least bit of ternary music—— No, gone!

I can't make my tongue conform to those accents,   25
for my visitor speaks – and so weightily, folks,
and so cheerfully, and the creep wears in turn
a panama hat, a cap, a helmet, a fez:

illustrations of various substantial arguments,
headgear in the sense of externalized thought?   30
Or maybe – oh, that would be really something
if thereby the clown indicated to me

that I kept changing countries like counterfeit money,
hurrying on and afraid to look back,
like a phantom dividing in two, like a candle   35
between mirrors sailing into the low sun.

It is far to the meadows where I sobbed in my childhood
having missed an Apollo, and farther yet
to the alley of firs where the midday sunlight
glowed with fissures of fire between bands of jet.   40

But my word, curved to form an aerial viaduct,
spans the world, and across in a strobe-effect spin
of spokes I keep endlessly passing incognito
into the flame-licked night of my native land.

To myself I appear as an idol, a wizard   45
bird-headed, emerald gloved, dressed in tights
made of bright-blue scales. I pass by. Reread it
and pause for a moment to ponder these lines.

Addressed to non-beings. Apropos, that shuffle
is no viaduct, but a procession of clouds,   50
and deprived of the simplest of possible blessings
(reaching up to the elbows, the temples, the eyes),

'Your poor books,' he breezily said, 'will finish
by hopelessly fading in exile. Alas,
those two thousand leaves of frivolous fiction   55
will be scattered; but genuine foliage has

a place where to fall: there's the soil, there's Russia,
there's a path drenched by maples in violet blood,
there's a threshold where lie overlapping gold aces,
60   there are ditches; but your unfortunate books

without soil, without path, without ditch, without
        threshold,
will be shed in a void where you brought forth a branch,
as bazaar fakirs do (that is, not without faking),
and not long will it bloom in the smoke-colored air.

65   Who, some autumn night, *who*, tell us, please, in the
        backwoods
of Russia, by lamplight, in his overcoat,
amidst cigarette gills, miscellaneous sawdust,
and other illumed indiscernibles – who

on the table a sample of *your* prose will open,
70   absorbed, will read *you* to the noise of the rain,
to the noise of the birch tree that rushes up window-ward
and to its own level raises the book?

No, never will anyone in the great spaces
make mention of even one page of your work;
75   the now savage will dwell in his savage ignorance,
friends of steppes won't forget their steppes for your sake.'

In a long piece of poetry, 'Fame', the author
is concerned, so to speak, with the problem, is irked
by the thought of contacting the reader's awareness . . .
80   'This too, I'm afraid, will vanish for good.

So repeat after me (as one rakes a delicious
sore to get to the end, to its heaven): Not once,
not once will my name come up briefly, save maybe
– as a star briefly passing among tragic clouds –

In a specialist's work, in a note to the title   85
of some *émigré* churchyard and on a par
with the names of my co-orthographical brethren
which a matter of locus had forced upon me.

Repeated? And furthermore, not without brio,
you happened to write in some quite foreign tongue.   90
You recall the particular anise-oil flavor
of those strainings, those flingings in verbal distress?

And a vision: you are in your country. Great writer.
Proud. Unyielding. But no one dares touch you. At times,
A translation or fragment. Admirers. All Europe   95
Esteems you. A villa near Yalta. A hero.'

2

Then I laugh, and at once from my pen nib a flight
    of my favorite anapests rises,
in the night making rocket streaks with the increase
    in the speed of the golden inscribing.   100

And I'm happy. I'm happy that Conscience, the pimp
    of my sleepy reflections and projects,
did not get at the critical secret. Today
    I am really remarkably happy.

That main secret tra-tá-ta tra-tá-ta tra-tá –   105
    and I must not be overexplicit;
this is why I find laughable the empty dream
    about readers, and body, and glory.

Without body I've spread, without echo I thrive,
    and with me all along is my secret.   110
A book's death can't affect me since even the break
    between me and my land is a trifle.

I admit that the night has been ciphered right well
  but in place of the stars I put letters,
and I've read in myself how the self to transcend –
  and I must not be overexplicit.

Trusting not the enticements of the thoroughfare
  or such dreams as the ages have hallowed,
I prefer to stay godless, with fetterless soul
  in a world that is swarming with godheads.

But one day while disrupting the strata of sense
  and descending deep down to my wellspring
I saw mirrored, besides my own self and the world,
  something else, something else, something else.

The Paris Poem

'Lead them off, only do not discard them!
They are human. Their Moscow they rue.
Give some thought to the needs of that scoundrel:
He was once an angel like you.

And extend a wing to Nicander,   5
Abram, Vladimir, and Leo, too;
to the slave, prince, traitor, bandit:
ils furent des anges comme vous.

The whole crew – at an alien fireside
(those ghastly necks of old men):   10
masters, my azure masters,
for my sake have pity on them!

2

From those wandering, those idly straying,
I now crawl away, and now rise,
and I'm flying at last – and "dissolving"   15
has no rhyme in my new paradise.

That is how by rank I'm entitled
with loud clangor to enter your hall.
Very well. I'm aware of the reason –
but they *must* be rescued all!   20

You at least might reflect, you at least might
condescend to glance briefly – Meanwhile
I remain your specterful (signature
illegible. Night. Cloudy sky).'

3

Thus he thought without willing it, weightless,
while into himself, like an heir, he flew.
The night breathed. The window drape billowed
with clouds paying clouds their due.

Chair. He on the chair. Bed. Upon it
he again. Mirror. He in its gulf.
He in the corner. He in the floor. At the finish.
In himself, in himself. Safe!

4

And now we begin. There dwelt in Paris,
number five on rue Pierre Loti,
one Vulf, a red-haired, lanky
civil engineer aged fifty-three.

And under him lived my hero, the author
whom I've written about more than once.
My pal, my employer.

5

Having looked at his watch and glimpsed
through the hour its pebble-strewn bottom,
he dressed and went out. He and I
dubbed that bottom: 'Ovidius
crammed with *carmina*.' Mist
and clods in the head after hideous
verse-making labor. A slight
drizzle outside, and above the black street
not the faintest star in the marron mist.
But there will be no poem: We've nowhere

to go. At night he would ramble.
He did not like visiting people
and did not know any nice animal.

6

To be one with this stone which is one with the night,
to drink this red wine, which the cabby drinks.
And the whores, they walk as the wagtails walk,
And the Russian Parnassus in darkness sinks.

Dying out are the shaggy mammoths,
barely alive is the red-eyed mouse.
Echoes of an illiterate lyre here wander,
from the slipshod to Boul'Mich you pass.

From a tongue half-Russian and half-forgotten
here you pass to a form of *argot*.
The pain of a severed vertebra wanders
in the black depths of Boulevard Arago.

Hasn't the very last inkdrop of Russia
already dried up? Let's be going then.
Yet we still attempt to scrawl our signature
with a crooked-beaked post-office pen.

7

Wondrous at night is gaunt Paris.
Hark! Under the vaults of black arcades,
where the walls are rocklike, the urinals
gurgle behind their shields.

There is Fate and an alpine something
in that desolate splash. Any moment now,
between even and odd, between me and non-me,
that keeper of records will choke and drown.

And the bridges! That's bliss everlasting,
the bliss of black water. Look, what a sight:
the vitrine of an incomparable pharmacy
80   and the globes of lamps full of orange light.

Overhead – matters there are less pretty
without end. Without end. Just a mist.
A dead moon phantasmed in its millpool.
Can it be that I too – ? Dismissed.

85   Death is distant yet (after tomorrow
I'll think everything through); but now and then
one's heart starts clamoring: Author! Author!
He is not in the house, gentlemen.

And while I looked at the crescent
90   as blue as a bruise, there came
from a distant suburb, the whistle
– heartrending sound! – of a train.

A huge clean sheet of paper I started
to extract from myself. The sheet
95   was bigger than me and frenetically
it rolled up in a funnel and creaked.

And the struggle began to seem muddled,
unresolvable: I, the black sky,
I, the lights, and the present minute –
100   and the present minute went by.

But who knows – perhaps, it was priceless
and perhaps I'd regret some day
having treated that sheet of paper
in such an inhuman way.

105   Perhaps something to me they incanted –
those stones and that whistle afar?
And on the sidewalk groping, my crumpled
scrap of paper I found in the dark.

8

In this life, rich in patterns (a life
unrepeatable, since with a different
cast, in a different manner,
in a new theater it will be given),

no better joy would I choose than to fold
its magnificent carpet in such a fashion
as to make the design of today coincide
with the past, with a former pattern,

in order to visit again – oh, not
commonplaces of those inclinations,
not the map of Russia, and not a lot
of nostalgic equivocations –

but, by finding congruences with the remote,
to revisit my fountainhead,
to bend and discover in my own childhood
the end of the tangled-up thread.

And carefully then to unravel myself
as a gift, as a marvel unfurled,
and become once again the middle point
of the many-pathed, loud-throated world.

And by the bright din of the birds
by the jubilant window-framed lindens
by their extravagant greenery,
by the sunlight upon me and in me,

by the white colossi that rush through the blue
straight at me – as I narrow my eyes –
by all that sparkle and all that power
my present moment to recognize.

110

115

120

125

130

135

No Matter How

No matter how the Soviet tinsel glitters
upon the canvas of a battle piece;
no matter how the soul dissolves in pity,
I will not bend, I will not cease

5   loathing the filth, brutality, and boredom
of silent servitude. No, no, I shout,
my spirit is still quick, still exile-hungry,
I'm still a poet, count me out!

On Rulers

You will (as sometimes
   people say)
laugh; you will (as clairvoyants
say) roar with laughter, gentlemen –
   but, word of honor,   5
   I have a crony,
      who
would be thrilled to shake hands
with the head of a state or of any other
      enterprise.   10

Since when, I wonder,
in the pit of the stomach
we've begun to experience a tender
bubbling, when looking through an opera glass
at the burly one, bristly haired, in the grand box?   15
   Since when the concept
of authority has been equated
with the seminal notion of patria?

All sorts of Romans and butchers;
Charles the Handsome and Charles the Hideous;   20
utterly rotten princelings; fat-breasted
German ladies; and various
cannibals, loverboys, lumbermen,
   Johns, Lewises, Lenins,
emitting stool grunts of strain and release,   25
   propping elbows on knees,
sat on their massive old thrones.

The historian dies of sheer boredom:
On the heels of Mamay comes another Mamay.
Does our plight really force us to do
    what did bureaucratic Cathay
that with heaps of superfluous centuries
augmented her limited history
(which, however, hardly became
    either better or merrier)?
Per contra, the coachmen of empires look good
when performing their duties: swiftly
toward them flies the blue of the sky;
their flame-colored sleeves clap in the wind;
the foreign observer looks on and sees
in front bulging eyes of great beauty
and behind a beautiful blend
of divan cushion and monstrous pumpkin.
But the decorated big fellow or else
    the trench-coated wolf
    in his army cap with a German steep peak,
    hoarse-voiced, his face all distorted,
    speaking from an immobile convertible,
or, again, a banquet
with Caucasian wine.
    No, thank you.

If my late namesake,
who used to write verse, in rank
and in file, at the very dawn
of the Soviet Small-Bourgeois order,
    had lived till its noon
he would be now finding taut rhymes
    such as 'praline'
      or 'air chill',
    and others of the same kind.

To Prince S. M. Kachurin

1

Kachurin, your advice I've accepted
and here I am, living for the third day
in a museumist setup: a blue
drawing room with a view on the Neva.

As an American clergyman   5
your poor friend is disguised,
and to all the Daghestan valleys
I send envious greetings.

Because of the cold, and the palpitations
of a false passport, I cannot sleep.   10
To wallpaper investigators
lianas and lilies I send.

But *he* sleeps (curled up on a canapé,
knees snugly pressed to the wall,
in a plaid rug wrapped up to the waist)   15
– the interpreter I've been assigned.

2

When last Sunday,
after the lapse of almost
thirty years of eclipse, I managed
to get up and walk as far as the window;   20

when I saw, in the mist
of spring and of the young day
and of muted outlines,
all that had been in my keeping

25 for so long – as a sort of too bright
picture postcard minus one corner
(cut off for the sake of the stamp
which had been in that corner);

when it all reappeared
30 so close to my soul,
my soul, emitting a sigh,
stopped like a train in the stillness of fields.

And I yearned to go off to the country:
with the languor of youth once more
35 my body dreamily ached
and I began to consider

how I'd sit in a railway carriage,
how I'd prevail upon him –
but here with slow smacks of lips he woke up
40 and reached for his dictionary.

3
On this I can't rest my case,
here explained is one's entire life
that has stopped like a train
in the rough-textured stillness of fields.

45 I imagine the twitter
at a distance of fifty
miles from the city,
from the house where, shut in, I stutter.

And the station, the slanting rain
seen against a dark background, and then   50
the petticoat toss of the station lilacs
already coarsening under the rain.

Next: the tarantass with its leathern lap cover
crossed by trembling trickles; and all
the details of the birch trees; and the red   55
barn to the left of the highway.

Yes, all the details, Kachurin,
all the poor little ones, such as
edge of dove-gray cloud, lozenge of azure,
stipple of tree trunk through ripple of leaves.   60

But how shall I take the local train,
wearing this coat, wearing these glasses
(and in point of fact completely translucent
with a novel of Sirin in my hands)?

4

I'm frightened. Neither the rostral column,   65
nor the steps that lead, under the moon,
down to the spiral reflections of lights,
to the compact quicksilver wave

can mask—— Anyway at our next meeting
I shall tell you everything   70
about the new, the broadshouldered
provincial and slave.

I want to go home. I've had enough.
Kachurin, may I go home?
To the pampas of my free youth,   75
to the Texas I once discovered.

I'm asking you: Isn't it time
to return to the theme of the bowstring,
or to what is enchantingly called 'chaparral'
in *The Headless Horseman*,

so as to fall asleep in Matagordo Gorge,
on the fiery-hot boulders there
with the skin of one's face parched by aquarelle paint,
and a crow's feather stuck in one's hair?

A Day Like Any Other

A day like any other. Memory dozed. A chilly
and dreary spring dragged on. Then, all at once,
a shadow at the bottom stirred
and from the bottom rose with sobs.

What's there to sob about? I'm a poor soother!   5
Yet how she stamps her feet, and shakes, and hotly
clings to my neck and in the dreadful darkness
begs to be gathered up, as babes are, in one's arms.

Irregular Iambics

For the last time, with leaves that flow
between the fingers of the air
and pass before the thunderstorm
from green by now importunate
into a simple silverness,
it ripples, the poor olive: foliage
of art! And it would seem that words
were now no longer worth the fondling,
had there not been a vagabond's
sharp-sightedness and approbation,
had not the gully held its lily,
had not the thunderstorm drawn near.

What Is the Evil Deed

What is the evil deed I have committed?
Seducer, criminal – is this the word
for me who set the entire world a-dreaming
   of my poor little girl?

Oh, I know well that I am feared by people: 5
They burn the likes of me for wizard wiles
and as of poison in a hollow smaragd
   of my art die.

Amusing, though, that at the last indention,
despite proofreaders and my age's ban,   10
a Russian branch's shadow shall be playing
   upon the marble of my hand.

From the Gray North

From the gray North
now come these photos.

Not all its arrears
life has had time to defray.
A familiar tree reappears
out of the gray.

This is the highway to Luga.
My house with the pillars. The Oredezh.
Almost from anywhere
homeward even today
I can still find my way.

Thus, sometimes, to the bathers
on the seaside sand
a small boy will bring over
something in his clenched hand.

Everything – from a pebble
with a violet rim
to the dim greenish part of a
glass object – is festively
brought over by him.

This is Batovo.
This is Rozhestveno.

The English Poems from
Poems and Problems

A Literary Dinner

Come here, said my hostess, her face making room
for one of those pink introductory smiles
that link, like a valley of fruit trees in bloom,
the slopes of two names.
I want you, she murmured, to eat Dr James.   5

I was hungry. The Doctor looked good. He had read
the great book of the week and had liked it, he said,
because it was powerful. So I was brought
a generous helping. His mauve-bosomed wife
kept showing me, very politely, I thought,   10
the tenderest bits with the point of her knife.
I ate – and in Egypt the sunsets were swell;
The Russians were doing remarkably well;
had I met a Prince Poprinsky, whom he had known
in Caparabella, or was it Mentone?   15
They had traveled extensively, he and his wife;
her hobby was People, his hobby was Life.
All was good and well cooked, but the tastiest part
was his nut-flavored, crisp cerebellum. The heart
resembled a shiny brown date,   20
and I stowed all the studs on the edge of my plate.

The Refrigerator Awakes

Crash!
And if darkness could sound, it would sound like this giant
waking up in the torture house, trying to die
and not dying, and trying
5   not to cry and immediately crying
that he will, that he will, that he will do his best
to adjust his dark soul to the pressing request
of the only true frost,
and he pants and he gasps and he rasps and he wheezes:
10   *ice is the solid form when the water freezes;*
a volatile liquid (see 'Refrigerating')
is permitted to pass into evaporating
coils, where it boils,
which somehow seems wrong,
15   *and I wonder how long*
it will rumble and shudder and crackle and pound;
Scudder, the Alpinist, slipped and was found
half a century later preserved in blue ice
with his bride and two guides and a dead edelweiss;
20   *a German has proved that the snowflakes we see*
are the germ cells of stars and the sea life to be;
hold
the line, hold the line, lest its tale be untold;
let it amble along through the thumping pain
25   *and horror of dichlordisomethingmethane,*
a trembling white heart with the frost froth upon it,
Nova Zembla, poor thing, with that B in her bonnet,
stunned bees in the bonnets of cars on hot roads,
Keep it Kold, says a poster in passing, and lo,
30   *loads,*
of bright fruit, and a ham, and some chocolate cream
and three bottles of milk, all contained in the gleam

of that wide-open white
god, the pride and delight
of starry-eyed couples in dream kitchenettes,   35
and it groans and it drones and it toils and it sweats –
Shackleton, pemmican, penguin, Poe's Pym –
collapsing at last in the criminal
night.

A Discovery

I found it in a legendary land
all rocks and lavender and tufted grass,
where it was settled on some sodden sand
hard by the torrent of a mountain pass.

The features it combines mark it as new
to science: shape and shade – the special tinge,
akin to moonlight, tempering its blue,
the dingy underside, the checquered fringe.

My needles have teased out its sculptured sex;
corroded tissues could no longer hide
that priceless mote now dimpling the convex
and limpid teardrop on a lighted slide.

Smoothly a screw is turned; out of the mist
two ambered hooks symmetrically slope,
or scales like battledores of amethyst
cross the charmed circle of the microscope.

I found it and I named it, being versed
in taxonomic Latin; thus became
godfather to an insect and its first
describer – and I want no other fame.

Wide open on its pin (though fast asleep),
and safe from creeping relatives and rust,
in the secluded stronghold where we keep
type specimens it will transcend its dust.

Dark pictures, thrones, the stones that pilgrims kiss,
poems that take a thousand years to die
but ape the immortality of this
red label on a little butterfly.

The Poem

Not the sunset poem you make when you think
                  aloud,
with its linden tree in India ink
and the telegraph wires across its pink
                  cloud;

not the mirror in you and her delicate bare
shoulder still glimmering there;
not the lyrical click of a pocket rhyme –
the tiny music that tells the time;

and not the pennies and weights on those
evening papers piled up in the rain;
not the cacodemons of carnal pain;
not the things you can say so much better in plain prose –

but the poem that hurtles from heights unknown
– when you wait for the splash of the stone
deep below, and grope for your pen,
and then comes the shiver, and then –

in the tangle of sounds, the leopards of words,
the leaflike insects, the eye-spotted birds
fuse and form a silent, intense,
mimetic pattern of perfect sense.

An Evening of Russian Poetry

*'. . . seems to be the best train. Miss Ethel Winter
of the Department of English will meet you at the
station and . . .'*

FROM A LETTER ADDRESSED
TO THE VISITING SPEAKER

The subject chosen for tonight's discussion
is everywhere, though often incomplete:
when their basaltic banks become too steep,
most rivers use a kind of rapid Russian,
and so do children talking in their sleep.   5
My little helper at the magic lantern,
insert that slide and let the colored beam
project my name or any such-like phantom
in Slavic characters upon the screen.
The other way, the other way. I thank you.   10

On mellow hills the Greek, as you remember,
fashioned his alphabet from cranes in flight;
his arrows crossed the sunset, then the night.
Our simple skyline and a taste for timber,
the influence of hives and conifers,   15
reshaped the arrows and the borrowed birds.
Yes, Sylvia?

            *'Why do you speak of words
when all we want is knowledge nicely browned?'*

Because all hangs together – shape and sound,
heather and honey, vessel and content.   20
Not only rainbows – every line is bent,
and skulls and seeds and all good worlds are round,

like Russian verse, like our colossal vowels:
those painted eggs, those glossy pitcher flowers
that swallow whole a golden bumblebee,
those shells that hold a thimble and the sea.
Next question.

'Is your prosody like ours?'

Well, Emmy, our pentameter may seem
to foreign ears as if it could not rouse
the limp iambus from its pyrrhic dream.
But close your eyes and listen to the line.
The melody unwinds; the middle word
is marvelously long and serpentine:
you hear one beat, but you have also heard
the shadow of another, then the third
touches the gong, and then the fourth one sighs.

It makes a very fascinating noise:
it opens slowly, like a greyish rose
in pedagogic films of long ago.

The rhyme is the line's birthday, as you know,
and there are certain customary twins
in Russian as in other tongues. For instance,
love automatically rhymes with blood,
nature with liberty, sadness with distance,
humane with everlasting, prince with mud,
moon with a multitude of words, but sun
and song and wind and life and death with none.

Beyond the seas where I have lost a scepter,
I hear the neighing of my dappled nouns,
soft participles coming down the steps,
treading on leaves, trailing their rustling gowns,
and liquid verbs in *ahla* and in *ili*,
Aonian grottoes, nights in the Altai,

black pools of sound with 'l's for water lilies.
The empty glass I touched is tinkling still, 55
but now 'tis covered by a hand and dies.

'Trees? Animals? Your favorite precious stone?'

The birch tree, Cynthia, the fir tree, Joan.
Like a small caterpillar on its thread,
my heart keeps dangling from a leaf long dead 60
but hanging still, and still I see the slender
white birch that stands on tiptoe in the wind,
and firs beginning where the garden ends
the evening ember glowing through their cinders.

Among the animals that haunt our verse, 65
that bird of bards, regale of night, comes first:
scores of locutions mimicking its throat
render its every whistling, bubbling, bursting,
flutelike or cuckoolike or ghostlike note.
But lapidary epithets are few; 70
we do not deal in universal rubies.
The angle and the glitter are subdued;
our riches lie concealed. We never liked
the jeweler's window in the rainy night.

My back is Argus-eyed. I live in danger. 75
False shadows turn to track me as I pass
and, wearing beards, disguised as secret agents,
creep in to blot the freshly written page
and read the blotter in the looking glass.
And in the dark, under my bedroom window, 80
until, with a chill whirr and shiver, day
presses its starter, warily they linger
or silently approach the door and ring
the bell of memory and run away.

Let me allude, before the spell is broken, 85
to Pushkin, rocking in his coach on long
and lonely roads: he dozed, then he awoke,

undid the collar of his traveling cloak,
and yawned, and listened to the driver's song.
90   Amorphous sallow bushes called *rakeety*,
enormous clouds above an endless plain,
songline and skyline endlessly repeated,
the smell of grass and leather in the rain.
And then the sob, the syncope (Nekrasov!),
95   the panting syllables that climb and climb,
obsessively repetitive and rasping,
dearer to some than any other rhyme.
And lovers meeting in a tangled garden,
dreaming of mankind, of untrammeled life,
100   mingling their longings in the moonlit garden,
where trees and hearts are larger than in life.
This passion for expansion you may follow
throughout our poetry. We want the mole
to be a lynx or turn into a swallow
105   by some sublime mutation of the soul.
But to unneeded symbols consecrated,
escorted by a vaguely infantile
path for bare feet, our roads were always fated
to lead into the silence of exile.

110   Had I more time tonight I would unfold
the whole amazing story – *neighuklúzhe*,
nevynossímo – but I have to go.

What did I say under my breath? I spoke
to a blind songbird hidden in a hat,
115   safe from my thumbs and from the eggs I broke
into the gibus brimming with their yolk.

And now I must remind you in conclusion,
that I am followed everywhere and that
space is collapsible, although the bounty
120   of memory is often incomplete:
once in a dusty place in Mora county
(half town, half desert, dump mound and mesquite)
and once in West Virginia (a muddy

red road between an orchard and a veil
of tepid rain) it came, that sudden shudder,   125
a Russian something that I could inhale
but could not see. Some rapid words were uttered
and then the child slept on, the door was shut.

The conjurer collects his poor belongings –
the colored handkerchief, the magic rope,   130
the double-bottomed rhymes, the cage, the song.
You tell him of the passes you detected.
The mystery remains intact. The check
comes forward in its smiling envelope.

'How would you say "delightful talk" in Russian?'   135
'How would you say "good night"?'

                    Oh, that would be:

Bessónnitza, tvoy vzor oonýl i stráshen;
lubóv moyá, otstóopnika prostée.

(Insomnia, your stare is dull and ashen,
my love, forgive me this apostasy.)   140

The Room

The room a dying poet took
at nightfall in a dead hotel
had both directories – the Book
of Heaven and the Book of Bell.

It had a mirror and a chair,
it had a window and a bed,
its ribs let in the darkness where
rain glistened and a shopsign bled.

Not tears, not terror, but a blend
of anonymity and doom,
it seemed, that room, to condescend
to imitate a normal room.

Whenever some automobile
subliminally slit the night,
the walls and ceiling would reveal
a wheeling skeleton of light.

Soon afterwards the room was mine.
A similar striped cageling, I
groped for the lamp and found the line
'Alone, unknown, unloved, I die'

in pencil, just above the bed.
It had a false quotation air.
Was it a she, wild-eyed, well-read,
or a fat man with thinning hair?

I asked a gentle Negro maid,   25
I asked a captain and his crew,
I asked the night clerk. Undismayed,
I asked a drunk. Nobody knew.

Perhaps when he had found the switch
he saw the picture on the wall   30
and cursed the red eruption which
tried to be maples in the fall?

Artistically in the style
of Mr Churchill at his best,
those maples marched in double file   35
from Glen Lake to Restricted Rest.

Perhaps my text is incomplete.
A poet's death is, after all,
a question of technique, a neat
enjambment, a melodic fall.   40

And here a life had come apart
in darkness, and the room had grown
a ghostly thorax, with a heart
unknown, unloved – but not alone.

Voluptates Tactionum

Some inevitable day
On the editorial page
Of your paper it will say,
'Tactio has come of age.'

When you turn a knob, your set
Will obligingly exhale
Forms, invisible and yet
Tangible – a world in Braille.

Think of all the things that will
Really be within your reach!
Phantom bottle, dummy pill,
Limpid limbs upon a beach.

Grouped before a Magnotact,
Clubs and families will clutch
Everywhere the same compact
Paradise (in terms of touch).

Palpitating fingertips
Will caress the flossy hair
And investigate the lips
Simulated in midair.

See the schoolboy, like a blind
Lover, frantically grope
For the shape of love – and find
Nothing but the shape of soap.

Restoration

To think that any fool may tear
by chance the web of when and where.
O window in the dark! To think
that every brain is on the brink
of nameless bliss no brain can bear,   5

unless there be no great surprise –
as when you learn to levitate
and, hardly trying, realize
– alone, in a bright room – that weight
is but your shadow, and you rise.   10

My little daughter wakes in tears:
She fancies that her bed is drawn
into a dimness which appears
to be the deep of all her fears
but which, in point of fact, is dawn.   15

I know a poet who can strip
a William Tell or Golden Pip
in one uninterrupted peel
miraculously to reveal,
revolving on his fingertip,   20

a snowball. So I would unrobe,
turn inside out, pry open, probe
all matter, everything you see,
the skyline and its saddest tree,
the whole inexplicable globe,   25

to find the true, the ardent core
as doctors of old pictures do
when, rubbing out a distant door
or sooty curtain, they restore
the jewel of a bluish view.

The Poplar

Before this house a poplar grows
Well versed in dowsing, I suppose,

But how it sighs! And every night
A boy in black, a girl in white

Beyond the brightness of my bed   5
Appear, and not a word is said.

On coated chair and coatless chair
They sit, one here, the other there.

I do not care to make a scene:
I read a glossy magazine.   10

He props upon his slender knee
A dwarfed and potted poplar tree.

And she – she seems to hold a dim
Hand mirror with an ivory rim

Framing a lawn, and her, and me   15
Under the prototypic tree,

Before a pillared porch, last seen
In July, nineteen seventeen.

This is the silver lining of
Pathetic fallacies: the sough   20

Of *Populus* that taps at last
Not water but the author's past.

And note: nothing is ever said.
I read a magazine in bed

25   Or the *Home Book of Verse*; and note:
This is my shirt, that is my coat.

But frailer seers I am told
Get up to rearrange a fold.

Lines Written in Oregon

Esmeralda! Now we rest
Here, in the bewitched and blest
Mountain forests of the West.

Here the very air is stranger.
Damzel, anchoret, and ranger   5
Share the woodland's dream and danger.

And to think I deemed you dead!
(In a dungeon, it was said;
Tortured, strangled); but instead –

Blue birds from the bluest fable,   10
Bear and hare in coats of sable,
Peacock moth on picnic table.

Huddled roadsigns softly speak
Of Lake Merlin, Castle Creek,
And (obliterated) Peak.   15

Do you recognize that clover?
Dandelions, *l'or du pauvre*?
(Europe, nonetheless, is over.)

Up the turf, along the burn,
Latin lilies climb and turn   20
Into Gothic fir and fern.

Cornfields have befouled the prairies
But these canyons laugh! And there is
Still the forest with its fairies.

25   And I rest where I awoke
In the sea shade – *l'ombre glauque* –
Of a legendary oak;

Where the woods get ever dimmer,
Where the Phantom Orchids glimmer –
30   Esmeralda, *immer, immer*.

Ode to a Model

I have followed you, model,
in magazine ads through all seasons,
from dead leaf on the sod
to red leaf on the breeze,

from your lily-white armpit   5
to the tip of your butterfly eyelash,
charming and pitiful,
silly and stylish.

Or in kneesocks and tartan
standing there like some fabulous symbol,   10
parted feet pointing outward
– pedal form of akimbo.

On a lawn, in a parody
Of Spring and its cherry tree,
near a vase and a parapet,   15
virgin practicing archery.

Ballerina, black-masked,
near a parapet of alabaster.
'Can one – somebody asked –
rhyme "star" and "disaster"?'   20

Can one picture a blackbird
as the negative of a small firebird?
Can a record, run backward,
turn 'repaid' into 'diaper'?

25   Can one marry a model?
     Kill your past, make you real, raise a family
     by removing you bodily
     from back numbers of Sham?

On Translating 'Eugene Onegin'

1

What is translation? On a platter
A poet's pale and glaring head,
A parrot's screech, a monkey's chatter,
And profanation of the dead.
The parasites you were so hard on   5
Are pardoned if I have your pardon,
O, Pushkin, for my stratagem:
I traveled down your secret stem,
And reached the root, and fed upon it;
Then, in a language newly learned,   10
I grew another stalk and turned
Your stanza patterned on a sonnet,
Into my honest roadside prose –
All thorn, but cousin to your rose.

2

Reflected words can only shiver   15
Like elongated lights that twist
In the black mirror of a river
Between the city and the mist.
Elusive Pushkin! Persevering,
I still pick up Tatiana's earring,   20
Still travel with your sullen rake.
I find another man's mistake,
I analyze alliterations
That grace your feasts and haunt the great
Fourth stanza of your Canto Eight.   25
This is my task – a poet's patience
And scholiastic passion blent:
Dove-droppings on your monument.

Rain

How mobile is the bed on these
nights of gesticulating trees
    when the rain clatters fast,
the tin-toy rain with dapper hoof
trotting upon an endless roof,
    traveling into the past.

Upon old roads the steeds of rain
Slip and slow down and speed again
    through many a tangled year;
but they can never reach the last
dip at the bottom of the past
    because the sun is there.

The Ballad of Longwood Glen

That Sunday morning, at half past ten,
Two cars crossed the creek and entered the glen.

In the first was Art Longwood, a local florist,
With his children and wife (now Mrs Deforest).

In the one that followed, a ranger saw   5
Art's father, stepfather and father-in-law.

The three old men walked off to the cove.
Through tinkling weeds Art slowly drove.

Fair was the morning, with bright clouds afar.
Children and comics emerged from the car.   10

Silent Art, who could stare at a thing all day,
Watched a bug climb a stalk and fly away.

Pauline had asthma, Paul used a crutch.
They were cute little rascals but could not run much.

'I wish,' said his mother to crippled Paul,   15
'Some man would teach you to pitch that ball.'

Silent Art took the ball and tossed it high.
It stuck in a tree that was passing by.

And the grave green pilgrim turned and stopped.
The children waited, but no ball dropped.   20

'I never climbed trees in my timid prime,'
Thought Art; and forthwith started to climb.

155

Now and then his elbow or knee could be seen
In a jigsaw puzzle of blue and green.

25 Up and up Art Longwood swarmed and shinned,
And the leaves said *yes* to the questioning wind.

What tiaras of gardens! What torrents of light!
How accessible ether! How easy flight!

His family circled the tree all day.
30 Pauline concluded: 'Dad climbed away.'

None saw the delirious celestial crowds
Greet the hero from earth in the snow of the clouds.

Mrs Longwood was getting a little concerned.
He never came down. He never returned.

35 She found some change at the foot of the tree.
The children grew bored. Paul was stung by a bee.

The old men walked over and stood looking up,
Each holding five cards and a paper cup.

Cars on the highway stopped, backed, and then
40 Up a rutted road waddled into the glen.

And the tree was suddenly full of noise,
Conventioners, fishermen, freckled boys.

Anacondas and pumas were mentioned by some,
And all kinds of humans continued to come:

45 Tree surgeons, detectives, the fire brigade.
An ambulance parked in the dancing shade.

A drunken rogue with a rope and a gun
Arrived on the scene to see justice done.

Explorers, dendrologists – all were there;
And a strange pale girl with gypsy hair.   50

And from Cape Fear to Cape Flattery
Every paper had: Man Lost in Tree.

And the sky-bound oak (where owls had perched
And the moon dripped gold) was felled and searched.

They discovered some inchworms, a red-cheeked gall,   55
And an ancient nest with a new-laid ball.

They varnished the stump, put up railings and signs.
Restrooms nestled in roses and vines.

Mrs Longwood, retouched, when the children died,
Became a photographer's dreamy bride.   60

And now the Deforests, with *four* old men,
Like regular tourists visit the glen;

Munch their lunches, look up and down,
Wash their hands, and drive back to town.

English Poems Not Included in *Poems and Problems*

Home

Music of windy woods, an endless song
Rippling in gleaming glades of Long Ago,
You follow me on tiptoe, swift and slow,
Through many a dreary year . . . Ah, it was wrong
To wound those gentle trees! I dream and roam   5
O'er sun-tormented plains, from brook to brook,
And thence by stone gray thundering cities. Home,
My home magnificent is but a word
On a withered page in an old, dusty book.
Oh, wistful birch trees! I remember days   10
Of beauty: ferns; a green and golden mare;
A toadstool like a giant lady bird;
A fairy path; bells, tinkling bells, and sighs;
Whimsical orioles; white-rimmed butterflies
Fanning their velvet wings on velvet silver stems . . .   15
All is dead. Who cares, who understands?
Not even God . . . I saw mysterious lands
And sailed to nowhere with blue-winged waves
Whirling around me. I have roved and raved
In southern harbors among drunken knaves,   20
And passed by narrow streets, scented and paved
With moonlight pale. There have I called and kissed
Veiled women swaying in a rhythmic mist,
But lonesome was my soul, and cold the night . . .
And if sometimes, when in the fading light   25
Chance friends would chatter, suddenly I grew
Restless and then quite still, – Ah, it was
Music of you, windy woods!

Remembrance

Like silent ships we two in darkness met,
    And when some day the poet's careless fame
    Shall breathe to you a half-forgotten name –
Soul of my song, I want you to regret.
For you had Love. Out of my life you tore
    One shining page. I want, if we must part,
    Remembrance pale to quiver in your heart
Like moonlit foam upon a windy shore.

The Russian Song

I dream of simple tender things:
a moonlit road and tinkling bells.
Ah, drearly the coachboy sings,
but sadness into beauty swells;

swells, and is lost in moonlight dim . . .   5
the singer sighs, and then the moon
full gently passes back to him
the quivering, unfinished tune.

In distant lands, on hill and plain,
thus do I dream, when nights are long, –   10
and memory gives back again
the whisper of that long-lost song.

Softest of Tongues

To many things I've said the word that cheats
the lips and leaves them parted (thus: *prash-chai*
which means 'good-bye') – to furnished flats, to streets,
to milk-white letters melting in the sky;
5   to drab designs that habit seldom sees,
to novels interrupted by the din
of tunnels, annotated by quick trees,
abandoned with a squashed banana skin;
to a dim waiter in a dimmer town,
10   to cuts that healed and to a thumbless glove;
also to things of lyrical renown
perhaps more universal, such as love.
Thus life has been an endless line of land
receding endlessly . . . And so that's that,
15   you say under your breath, and wave your hand,
and then your handkerchief, and then your hat.
To all these things I've said the fatal word,
using a tongue I had so tuned and tamed
that – like some ancient sonneteer – I heard
20   its echoes by posterity acclaimed.
But now thou too must go; just here we part,
softest of tongues, my true one, all my own . . .
And I am left to grope for heart and art
and start anew with clumsy tools of stone.

Exile

He happens to be a French poet, that thin,
book-carrying man with a bristly gray chin;
      you meet him wherever you go
across the bright campus, past ivy-clad walls.
The wind which is driving him mad (this recalls   5
      a rather good line in Hugo),
keeps making blue holes in the waterproof gloss
of college-bred poplars that rustle and toss
      their slippery shadows at pied
young beauties, all legs, as they bicycle through   10
his shoulder, his armpit, his heart, and the two
      big books that are hurting his side.

Verlaine had been also a teacher. Somewhere
in England. And what about great Baudelaire,
      alone in his Belgian hell?   15
This ivy resembles the eyes of the deaf.
Come, leaf, name a country beginning with 'f';
      for instance, 'forget' or 'farewell'.
Thus dimly he muses and dreamily heeds
his eavesdropping self as his body recedes,   20
      dissolving in sun-shattered shade.
L'Envoi: Those poor chairs in the Bois, one of which
legs up, stuck half-drowned in the slime of a ditch
      while others were grouped in a glade.

A Poem

When he was small, when he would fall,
on sand or carpet he would lie
quite flat and still until he knew
what he would do: get up or cry.

5   After the battle, flat and still
upon a hillside now he lies –
but there is nothing to decide,
for he can neither cry nor rise.

Dream

'Now it is coming, and the sooner
the better', said my swooning soul –
and in the sudden blinding lunar
landscape, out of a howling hole

a one-legged child that howled with laughter   5
hopped and went hopping hopping after
a bloody and bewildered bone,
a limb that walked away alone.

Perhaps the window shade had billowed
and slapped the darkness on the face;   10
but when I had picked up and pillowed
the book of sleep and found the place,

I saw him haltingly returning
out of the dust, back to the burning
hole of his three-walled home – that boy   15
hugging a new, a nameless toy.

Dandelions

Moons on the lawn replace the suns
that mowers happily had missed,
Where age would stoop, a babe will squat
and rise with star-fluff in its fist.

Lunar Lines

Spell 'night'. Spell 'pebbles': Pebbles in the Night.
Peep, crated chicks on lonely station! This
Is now the ABC of the abyss,
The Desperanto we must learn to write.

Notes

In what follows, my notes, which are mainly bibliographic, are printed alongside those of Vladimir and Dmitri Nabokov from various earlier publications. Vladimir Nabokov's notes from *Poems and Problems* (New York: McGraw-Hill, 1970) – abbreviated to *PP* below – are reproduced exactly as they appear in that edition, although the footnotes have here become endnotes (as have Dmitri Nabokov's), and any incorrect bibliographic details have been corrected. In the notes below, the date and place of composition are given for each poem, along with the source of that information (placed in brackets), where a source exists for these details. This is followed by the publication history of the poem. Where Dmitri Nabokov's translations appeared previously, I have given details of their earlier publication. Unless otherwise stated, Vladimir Nabokov's English translations of the Russian poems in *Poems and Problems* first appeared in that volume. For all poems originally written in Russian the date of composition refers to the original Russian version, not the translation.

In compiling notes on bibliographic and compositional history, I have benefited a great deal from Michael Juliar's *Vladimir Nabokov: A Descriptive Bibliography* (New York: Garland, 1986), from the notes to Nabokov's five-volume *Sobranie sochinenii sochinenii russkogo perioda* (*Collected Works of the Russian Period*) (St Petersburg: Symposium, 1999–2000), and especially from Maria Malikova's Russian edition of the poems, *Stikhotvoreniia* (*Poems*) (St Petersburg: Akademicheskii proekt, 2002). I have, however, done my best to verify the bibliographic details, and where necessary correct them, by consulting the archives of *Rul'* (the *Rudder*), the *New Yorker*, and other journals, and by checking the manuscripts in the Berg Collection of the New York Public Library. In some cases it has not been possible to check these details, as with poems first published in *Russkoe ekho* (*Russian Echo*). I did not have access to Nabokov's letters to his mother and wife, and where details of the poems come from these archives, I have had to rely on Malikova's research. Where a previous publication, such as the *Stikhi* (*Poems*) of 1979 or Malikova's 2002 edition, gives a composition date that I have not been able to verify from manuscript, I have put the name of that publication in brackets as the source. Malikova sometimes specifies her source for the dating, such as a letter from Nabokov, and in these cases I have reproduced her description of that source. Caution should be also taken over the compositional dates of some of the early poems, where it is often not clear whether the dates at the bottom of manuscripts correspond to the pre-revolutionary Julian or to the post-revolutionary Gregorian calendar. Where two alternative dates are given, separated by a diagonal slash, the first is the date according to the Julian (pre-revolutionary) calendar, the second the Gregorian date.

Many of Nabokov's Russian poems were first published in *Rul'*, the émigré newspaper of which his father had been one of the founding editors, or in one of the other émigré periodicals, such as *Segodnia* (*Today*), *Russkoe ekho*, *Poslednie novosti* (the *Latest News*) or *Sovremennye zapiski* (*Contemporary Annals*), the 'thick journal' which published *The University Poem* and many of his novels. In America, Nabokov continued to publish in Russian émigré journals, such as the New York publication *Novyi zhurnal* (the *New Review*). His English-language poems written in America appeared mainly in the *New Yorker* and the *Atlantic Monthly*. Some of the Russian poems which were published in journals, but had not been included in the book collections that appeared during Nabokov's lifetime, appeared in the 1979 *Stikhi*. Since then, the two landmark publications of the five-volume *Sobranie sochinenii* and of Malikova's *Stikhotvoreniia* – abbreviated to 'Malikova' below – have made available the vast majority (though not all) of Nabokov's previously published Russian poetry. Malikova's edition also reprinted the nine English poems which had not appeared in the two volumes of Nabokov's English verse that appeared in his lifetime, *Poems* (1959) and *Poems and Problems* (1970).

Nabokov made various changes to his poems as they passed from manuscript to journal publication, to the book collections of the émigré years, and then into the various book collections published after the Second World War. This is not a full scholarly edition, and I have not listed every change in punctuation, but I have noted those textual variants which seem to me particularly significant and interesting. In the case of the Russian poems, these variants will be of use to readers with a knowledge of Russian who can check the Russian texts in the various Russian editions (the 1979 *Stikhi*, the *Sobranie sochinenii*, and Malikova's edition of the *Stikhotvoreniia*); in the case of the poems in English, they can be checked against the text printed in this volume. Many of Nabokov's poems and stanzas of the 1920s ended either with the dying fall of an ellipsis or with the formalized passion of an exclamation mark – both of which devices have a long history in Russian as in English verse. In the 1952 *Stikhotvoreniia* and in *Poems and Problems*, Nabokov often modernized his poems by replacing these devices with a simple full stop. This process went further in *Stikhi*; mostly, it seems, without Nabokov's involvement. The editors of the modern Russian editions have also frequently printed versions of the poems in which punctuation has been silently modernized. Such changes considerably alter the feeling and meaning of the poems, however, and it is particularly in these cases that I have noted the alterations. There are also certain changes in wording which I have noted.

I have followed Malikova in quoting (in my translation from the Russian) from some remarks Nabokov gave about his poems at a 1949 reading, the text of which is reproduced as *Zametki 'Dlia avtorskogo vechera 7 Maia 1949 goda'* (*Notes 'Towards an Evening with the Author 7 May 1949'*) in *V. V. Nabokov: Pro et Contra* (*V. V. Nabokov: For and Against*) (St Petersburg: Russkii Khristianskii gumanitarnyi institut, 2001), vol. 2, pp. 124–44 (abbreviated to *Zametki* below). I have also followed Malikova in including information about composition drawn from Nabokov's letters to Edmund Wilson, collected by Simon Karlinsky in *Dear Bunny – Dear Volodya* (Berkeley: University of California Press, 2001) – shortened to *Dear Bunny* below – and from Nabokov's *Selected Letters, 1940–1977*, edited by Dmitri Nabokov and Matthew Bruccoli (San Diego: Harcourt Brace Jovanovich, 1989).

Poems Translated by Dmitri Nabokov

Music [*Muzyka*] (p. 5)

Dated summer 1914, Vyra (northern Russia), the Nabokov country estate (manuscript). The Russian text is hitherto unpublished; this translation is published here for the first time.

Revolution [*Revoliutsiia*]
(p. 6)

Dated 1917. The text is taken from the manuscript of Kornei Chukovskii's *Chukokkala*, first published in 1979, but was not in the published version of that text. It was first printed by E. Ts. Chukovskii

in *Nashe nasledie* (*Our Heritage*) 4 (1989), p. 71. This translation
first appeared in the *Paris Review* 175 (Fall/Winter 2005), pp. 171–3.

Peter in Holland [*Petr v Gollandii*]
(p. 7)

Dated 17 March 1919 (manuscript). First published in *The Empyrean
Path* (1923), where there is a dash before the fifth line that does not
appear in Malikova. This translation first appeared in the *Naboko-
vian* 51 (Fall 2003), p. 4, with the following note appended to it by
Dmitri Nabokov:

> 'Carpenter' refers to Peter's use of the assumed trade and name 'Plotnik
> [carpenter] Peter Mikhailov' when he entered Holland during the so-called
> Grand Embassy. It should also be noted that one of the main reasons for
> Peter's going to Holland was the study of shipbuilding – which of course
> was still mostly carpentry in the late 17th Century – in view of creating
> a Russian navy.

The Last Supper [*Tainaia vecheria*]
(p. 8)

Dated 12 June 1920 (manuscript); 1918, Crimea (*Stikhi*). First pub-
lished in *Rul'* 136 (29 April 1921), p. 2; republished in *The Empyrean
Path* (1923) and in *Stikhi* (1979). This translation first appeared in
the *Nabokovian* 60 (Spring 2008), pp. 6–7. In the version published
in *The Empyrean Path*, the first, second, and fifth lines end with
ellipses.

Easter [*Paskha*]
(p. 9)

First published in *Rul'* 431 (16 April 1922), p. 10, without the dedi-
cation. Republished in *The Cluster* (1922), also without the dedication,
and in *Stikhi* (1979), where the dedication is included. This transla-
tion first appeared in *Areté* 13 (Winter 2003), pp. 12–13. The poem
is dedicated to Nabokov's father, Vladimir Dmitrievich Nabokov, who
was killed on 28 March 1922 by a monarchist assassin during a
botched attempt on the life of another man, Paul Milyukov.

The Ruler [*Vlastitelin*]
(p. 10)

First published in *Segodnia* 72 (8 April 1923), p. 5; republished in *Stikhi* (1979), where the title was removed. This translation first appeared in the *Nabokovian* 24 (Spring 1990), pp. 46–9. It is republished here with revisions. In the manuscript, the second and eighth lines end with exclamation marks. The date of composition is given in *Stikhi* and Malikova as 7 December 1923. Given the publication date, this must be an error.

The Glasses of St Joseph [*Ochki Iosifa*]
(p. 11)

First published in *Rul'* 739 (6 May 1923), p. 2, where it is one of a number of poems grouped under the title '*Gekzametry*' ('Hexameters'). This translation first appeared in the *Nabokovian* 54 (Spring 2005), p. 4.

'Like pallid dawn, my poetry sounds gently'
[*'Kak blednaia zaria, moi stikh negromok'*]
(p. 12)

Dated 31 August 1923 (*Stikhi*). First published in *Stikhi* (1979). This translation first appeared in the *Nabokovian* 43 (Fall 1999), pp. 16–17.

Shakespeare [*Shekspir*]
(p. 13)

Dated 28 February 1924 in two manuscripts, where in both cases the title given is '*Posle chteniia Shekspira*' ('After Reading Shakespeare'). First published in *Zhar-Ptitsa* (the *Fire-Bird*) 12 (1924), p. 32; republished in *Stikhi* (1979). This translation first appeared in the *Nabokovian* 20 (Spring 1988), pp. 15–16. It is republished here with 'Will' for 'will' in line 20; 'their trace' for 'there trace' in line 37; 'Brantôme' for 'Brantome' in line 38; 'unashamèd' for 'unashamed' in line 45; and 'then, in the distance, smiling, vanished' for 'then vanished in the distance, smiling' in line 48. In the Russian version in both

175

manuscripts, the seventh line has '*khitro*' ('cunningly') for '*legko*' ('easily') in the printed version.

Cubes [*Kuby*]
(p. 15)

First published in *Rul'* 992 (9 March 1924), p. 2; republished in *Stikhi* (1979). This translation is published here for the first time.

St Petersburg [*Sankt-Peterburg*]
(p. 16)

Dated 26 May 1924, Berlin (*Stikhi*). First published in *Rul'* 1061 (1 June 1924), p. 2; republished in *Stikhi* (1979). This translation first appeared in the *Nabokovian* 42 (Spring 1999), pp. 6–8, with the following notes appended to it by Dmitri Nabokov:

> This poem is characterized by playful variations of rhyme scheme and line ending: strophes One and Three have a traditional *abab*, FMFM structure, while strophe Two has *abba*, FMMF, and strophe Four *abba*, MFFM. The translation preserves the rhythm of the original, and, where possible, attempts its rhymes.

> [Line 1] *Leila*. 'A name of Arabian origin that figures in Persian and other legends, but is used here in a generically romantic sense. As in the Russian, the stress should fall on the i, pronounced e.'

> [Line 5] *boundary eagles*. 'Eagle-like ornaments topped the metal fence along one side of the Summer Garden.'

> [Line 8] *Pushkin on the granite*. 'Is the parapet on the Neva quay, which the Summer Garden adjoined. See also VN's 1937 lecture/essay "Pushkin or the real and the plausible", pub. in English in *NYRB* [*New York Review of Books*], 31 March 1988.'

> [Line 12] *that floating signboard*. 'On the Fontanka, a tributary of the Neva that bordered the Summer Garden at right angles to the larger river, fish was sold from permanently moored barges (and kept alive in underwater cages accessible through a rectangular aperture in the boat's deck). The reference here is probably to an advertisement atop such a vessel.'

> [Line 16] *golden dust*. 'Dry, pulverized horse dung.'

Evening [*Vecher*]
(p. 17)

Dated 10 July 1924 (manuscript). First published in *Stikhi* (1979). This translation first appeared in *Areté* 13 (Winter 2003), pp. 16–17. An earlier version of the translation was published in *The Achievements of Vladimir Nabokov*, edited by G. Gibian and S. J. Parker (Ithaca, NY: Cornell University Press, 1984), pp. 168–9.

Fortune-telling [*Gadan'e*]
(p. 18)

First published in *Segodnia* (26 August 1924), p. 11; republished in *Stikhi* (1979). This translation first appeared in the *Nabokovian* 43 (Fall 1999), p. 44, with the following note appended to it by Dmitri Nabokov:

> The dreamy description of a Russian fortune-telling ritual, one of whose features was the course taken in a water-filled basin by half a walnut shell containing a miniature candle. The Svetlana ['Illuminated'] of this poem is generic, a name whose music suits the atmosphere. It probably echoes Zhukovski's romantic heroine more than it does a fiancée with whom Nabokov's relationship had ended the previous year.

The Demon [*Demon*]
(p. 20)

Dated 27 September 1924, Berlin (*Stikhi*). First published *Russkoe ekho* 74 (4 January 1925) under the title '*Demon*'; republished, without a title, in *Stikhi* (1979). This translation, by Dmitri Nabokov, first appeared in the *Nabokovian* 28 (Spring 1992), pp. 34–5. An earlier translation, by Joseph Brodsky, was published in the *Kenyon Review* (New Series) 1, no. 1 (Winter 1979), p. 120. The version in *Russkoe ekho* has no division into stanzas and a different wording in the final line: '*Mne Bog velit zvuchat*'' for '*Mne Bog velel zvuchat*'' – that is, 'God orders me to sound' (as in the translation published here) for 'God ordered me to sound' (Malikova).

The Skater [*Kon'kobezhets*]
(p. 21)

First published in *Rul'* 1269 (5 February 1925), p. 2; republished in *Stikhi* (1979). This translation first appeared in *Areté* 13 (Winter 2003), pp. 16–17. It is republished here with 'image' for 'illustration' in line 8 and 'by that melodious whistling' for 'with that melodious whistling' in line 11.

Spring [*Vesna*]
(p. 22)

First published in *Rul'* 1348 (10 May 1925), p. 2; republished in *The Return of Chorb* (1929) and in *Stikhi* (1979). This translation first appeared in the *Nabokovian* 28 (Spring 1992), pp. 36–9. In the version published in *Chorb*, there is a full stop at the end of the third line; a dash at the start of line 7; a dash after '*teper*'' in line 10; a dash after '*usad'be*' in line 15; no dash after line 19; a semicolon instead of a dash at the end of line 21; a full stop instead of a colon at the end of line 30; and a dash after '*obratnoi*' in line 32.

Dream [*Son*]
(p. 24)

First published in *Rul'* 1389 (30 June 1925), p. 2; republished in *Stikhi* (1979). This translation first appeared in *Areté* 13 (Winter 2003), p. 9.

The Train Wreck [*Krushenie*]
(p. 25)

First published in *Rul'* 1430 (16 August 1925), p. 7; republished in *The Return of Chorb* (1929) and in *Stikhi* (1979). This translation first appeared in the *Nabokovian* 22 (Spring 1989), pp. 12–17. In the version published in *Chorb*, there is a comma after '*bagazhnyi*' in line 5; a comma at the end of line 8; a semicolon at the end of line 14; a dash at the end of line 21; an ellipsis at the end of line 25; a dash after '*vot*' in line 26; an ellipsis after '*zhalost*'' in line 29; an ellipsis after '*son*' in line 32; a semicolon after '*rychag*' in line 38; a comma and a dash after *zhe* in line 41, and a comma and a dash after *krylatyi* in the same line.

Ut Pictura Poesis
(p. 27)

The title of the Russian text is given in Roman, not Cyrillic, script. First published in *Rul'* 1640 (25 April 1926), p. 2; republished in *Stikhi* (1979). This translation first appeared in the *Nabokovian* 51 (Fall 2003), pp. 28–31; republished in *Areté* 13 (Winter 2003), pp. 14–15. The poem is dedicated to M. V. Dobuzhinsky, a painter who had been Nabokov's art teacher in boyhood, and who designed the sets for the New York production of Nabokov's play *The Event* (1941). The title is the Latin for 'as is painting, so is poetry', a statement from Horace's *Ars Poetica*, which has become a conventional formula used about literature that aspires to resemble painting.

A Trifle [*Pustiak*]
(p. 28)

Composed 17–18 June 1926, the Black Forest (Malikova, basing her date on a letter from Nabokov to his wife Véra of 18 June). First published, without a title, in *Zveno* (the *Link*) (Paris) 179 (4 July 1926), p. 7; republished in *Stikhi* (1979), also without a title. This translation is published here for the first time, with a title added by Dmitri Nabokov.

The University Poem [*Universitetskaia poema*]
(p. 29)

Composed towards the end of 1926. First published in *Sovremennye zapiski* (Paris) 33 (1927), pp. 223–54. This translation is published here for the first time, with the following note appended to it by Dmitri Nabokov:

> The University Poem is based on VN's experiences at Trinity College, Cambridge, which he attended from 1919 to 1922.
> The poem is fundamentally a tribute to Pushkin. It consists, like *Eugene Onegin*, of 63 14-line stanzas and is written in iambic tetrameter.

Its character, however, is very different. The antique town of Cambridge, practically to this day, is basically unchanged, as are many of the customs of the college. The small suite of rooms where VN lived, and where I lodged when participating in a Nabokov Festival at Cambridge, is very much as it was in my father's day. An important change, however, was the disappearance of the black-clad little crones who would enter quietly to light the morning fire, and put the rooms in order when the students went off to class. Even the local girls were repetitious. Every year they would encounter a new suitor, knowing full well that the fling was going to be temporary and that next year a replacement beau would come along. Violet, whom our student meets at the vicar's tea, and with whom he has a brief romance, seems destined for the same kind of bittersweet, menial, uncertain future – rejecting a succession of suitors, awaiting next year's crop. Meanwhile, Violet's best years were passing. Besides this touching theme, there are many other charming nuances; then, in a quite different tone, comes the unexpected virtuoso conclusion:

> Before our parting I ask only one thing:
> as you fly, swallowlike, now lower,
> now on high, find one plain word within this world,
> always swift to understand you,
> where moth and rust do not corrupt,
> cherishing each instant,
> blessing each motion,
> do not allow it to freeze still,
> perceive the delicate rotation
> of the slightly tilted earth.

A word is in order regarding certain principles of poetic translation. As he did in his original prose and poetic writings, Vladimir Nabokov experimented, over the years, with various solutions in translating a poetic line. There, too, certain references and allusions are easily recognizable, while others are distant and abstruse. Some range from an accurate reproduction of meter and rhyme scheme, with less attention devoted to precision of meaning, to an unwavering, undaunted fidelity to the author's sense. The latter approach represents the essence of Nabokov's translation of Pushkin's *Eugene Onegin*. The purpose of that translation was to provide a faithful version for the purpose of teaching Nabokov's Cornell classes. It was, as he explained on many occasions, a 'pony' in which English locutions reproduced the Russian as closely as possible, even if that meant using difficult words to express complex ideas. Nabokov's explanations failed to protect him from attacks from many quarters, ranging from the eminent critic Edmund Wilson to a more recent criticule named Hofstadter.

In this translation, I have adhered to Nabokovian principles with regard to prosody as well. That means I have dispensed with rhymes (unless they happened to fall into my lap) and exact meter, while maintaining, nevertheless, a semblance of poetic rhythm.

[Stanza 11, line 13, *Calliope*] The muse of epic poems, eldest of the muses.

[Stanza 22, line 11, *keeps falling all the time, poor chap*] The 'Poor chap' is obviously the goalkeeper, lunging at the oncoming ball (Violet's knowledge of the game is limited).

[Stanza 45, line 9, *'Alla verdy'*] An old Russian military song.

Butterflies [*Babochki*]
(p. 55)

The poem from which this is an extract, *'Babochki'*, was never published. It was written 1926–9 and sent to the lepidopterist Nikolai Kardakov. This translation first appeared in *Nabokov's Butterflies*, edited by Brian Boyd and Robert Michael Pyle (Boston: Beacon Press, 2000), p. 121, with corrections to the translation in the second printing.

Tolstoy [*Tolstoi*]
(p. 56)

In the manuscript there is a handwritten note stating that this poem was read in Berlin on 4 September 1928 at an event marking the centenary of Tolstoy's birth. First published in *Rul'* 2374 (16 September 1928), p. 2. This translation first appeared in the *New York Review of Books* 35, no. 3 (3 March 1988), p. 6. In the typescript of the Russian text there is a stanza break after the eleventh line.

'I have no need, for my nocturnal travels'
[*'Dlia stranstviia nochnogo mne ne nado'*]
(p. 59)

Dated 20 July 1929 (Malikova). First published in *Rul'* 2647 (11 August 1929), p. 2; republished in *Stikhi* (1979). This translation first appeared in the *Nabokovian* 40 (Spring 1998), pp. 8–11. It is republished here, with 'I am set' for 'I'm all set' in line 4.

To the Grapefruit [*Pomplimusu*]
(p. 61)

Dated 24 January 1931 (manuscript). First published in *Sovremennye zapiski* 47 (1931), p. 233; republished in *Stikhi* (1979). This translation first appeared in the *Nabokovian* 42 (Spring 1999), pp. 38–9.

The Hawkmoth
(p. 62)

This is the fourth in a suite of seven untitled Russian poems, called collectively '*Sem' stikhotvoreniia*' ('Seven Poems'), which Nabokov composed in 1953. The whole sequence was published in *Novyi zhurnal* 46 (1956), pp. 43–6. This poem appears on pp. 44–5. The sequence was republished in *Stikhi* (1979). This translation is published here for the first time, with a title added by Dmitri Nabokov.

'Forty-three years, forty-four years maybe'
[*'Sorok tri ili chetyre goda'*]
(p. 63)

Dated 9 April 1967 (*Stikhi* and Malikova, who cites as authority for the date a manuscript with this date, sent in a letter to Roman Grinberg). First published in *Vozdushnye puti* (*Aerial Ways*) (New York) 5 (1967); republished in *Stikhi* (1979). This translation first appeared in the *Nabokovian* 40 (Spring 1998), pp. 12–13.

To Véra
(p. 64)

The poem is dedicated to Nabokov's wife, Véra. Dated 1 October 1974, Montreux (*Stikhi*). First published in *Stikhi* (1979). This translation first appeared in the *Nabokovian* 23 (Fall 1989), pp. 13–4, with the following note appended to it by Dmitri Nabokov:

> Nabokov had just completed *Look at the Harlequins!* and the novel would be published [. . .] on 27 August, 1974. He speculates on its fate if it ever reaches Soviet shores. The poem is constructed somewhat jocularly around two key rhymes, particularly *rombam – aplombom* in the second

verse. A little trickery was required to render the imagined Soviet review while preserving the feminine line ending and a semblance of that rhyme, which requires that 'rhombi' be pronounced, in one variant of the Latin manner, 'rombé,' and that 'aplomb' conserve at least a *soupçon* of its B.

The Russian Poems from *Poems and Problems*

The Rain Has Flown [*Dozhd' proletel*]
(p. 67)

Dated May 1917, Vyra (northern Russia) (*PP*). First published in *Al'manakh: dva puti* (*An Almanac: Two Paths*) (Petrograd, 1918) (*PP*); republished in *Stikhi* (1979). In the typescript the poem lacks the indentations of the even lines of the version as printed in *PP*. Nabokov describes the composition of this poem in the eleventh chapter of his autobiography, *Speak, Memory* (1951; extended version 1966), where he projects it back to the summer of 1914 and says it was his first poem. In fact he had been writing poetry for several years, as 'Music' (actually composed in 1914) shows. The following note is appended by Nabokov in *PP*:

> The phrase *letit dozhd'*, 'rain is flying,' was borrowed by the author from an old gardener (described in *Speak, Memory*, Chapter Two *et passim*) who applied it to light rain soon followed by sunshine. The poem was composed in the park of our country place in the last spring my family was to spend there. It was first published in *Dva Puti*, a collection of juvenile poems (a schoolmate's and mine), in Petrograd, January 1918, and was set to music by the composer Vladimir Ivanovich Pohl at Yalta, early 1919.

To Liberty [*K svobode*]
(p. 68)

Dated 3/16 December 1917 Gaspra (Crimea) (*PP*). This is the day on which Nabokov's father arrived with the latest political news. First published in *PP* (1970). In the manuscript the title of this poem is '*Svobode*', and there is a variant in the fifth line, with '*krylami nad-lomlennym*' ('with broken wings') for '*krylo podbitoe*' ('with injured/broken wing') in the printed version. The following note is appended by Nabokov in *PP*:

The main – and, indeed, only – interest of these lines resides in their revealing the disappointment of the intelligentsia, who had welcomed the liberal Revolution of the spring of 1917 and was distressed by the Bolshevist insurrection in the autumn of the same year. The fact of that reactionary regime having now survived for more than half a century adds a prophetic touch to a young poet's conventional poem. It may have been published in 1918, in some Yalta newspaper, but was not included in any of my later collections.

I Still Keep Mute [*Eshchyo bezmolvstvuiu*]
(p. 69)

Dated 23 March 1919 (manuscript); 4 April 1919, Livadia (Crimea) (*PP*). First published in *The Empyrean Path*, where there is no title; republished in *PP* and *Stikhi* (1979) with its title. In *The Empyrean Path*, there is a dash after '*bezmol'stvuiu*' in line 1 (removed in *PP*); a dash after '*gorniia*' in line 4; a comma after '*dal*' in line 6; and a semi-colon at the end of line 6. In two manuscript versions of the Russian poem, for '*i krepnu v tishine*' in the first line, *The Empyrean Path* and *PP* have '*i krepnu ia v tishe*' (both versions translatable as 'and in the hush grow strong'). Where the manuscripts have '*v dushevoi glubine*' ('in the depths of my soul'), *The Empyrean Path* and *PP* have '*vo mgle moei dushi*' ('in the shadows of my soul'). A third manuscript follows the wording of the other two manuscripts, but with the words crossed out and the wording of the published version written above.

Hotel Room [*Nomer v gostinitse*]
(p. 70)

Dated the night of 26/27 March 1919 (manuscript); in *PP* Nabokov notes the date and location as 8 April 1919, room 7, Hotel Metropole, Sebastopol '(a few days before leaving Russia)'. First published in *PP* (1970); republished in *Stikhi* (1979). In the manuscript, the poem concludes with an ellipsis, whereas in *PP* and in *Stikhi* there is a full stop.

Provence [*Provans*]
(p. 71)

Dated 19 August 1923, Solliès-Pont (*PP*). First published in *Rul'* 839 (2 September 1923), p. 2. This is the second half of the poem entitled

'*Provans*', as it was published in *Rul'*. This part was titled '*Solntse*' ('The Sun') when it was published in *The Return of Chorb* (1929).

La Bonne Lorraine
(p. 72)

Dated 6 September 1924, Berlin (Malikova, on the basis of a manuscript included in a letter Nabokov sent to his mother on that date). First published in *Rul'* 1151 (16 September 1924), p. 2, under the title 'La Belle Lorraine' (in Roman script). In the manuscript the title was originally given as 'La Belle Lorraine'; 'Belle' is crossed out and the word 'Bonne' written above it. Republished in *The Return of Chorb* (1929), where there is a comma after '*zdes*' in line 5; a comma after '*rez'boiu*' in line 9; and a comma after '*zabralo*' in line 13.

The Blazon [*Gerb*]
(p. 73)

Dated 24 January 1925, Berlin (*PP*, and Malikova, who cites the manuscript of the poem enclosed in a letter Nabokov wrote to his mother on that date). First published in *Russkoe ekho* (1 March 1925).

The Mother [*Mat'*]
(p. 74)

First published in *Rul'* 1330 (19 April 1925), p. 2; republished in *The Return of Chorb* (1929). In *Chorb*, there is an ellipsis after '*tomlen'e*' in line 9; a comma after '*groba*' in line 14; a comma after '*den*' in line 14; an ellipsis at the end of line 18; a comma after '*proplyvaiut*" in line 21; a comma and dash after '*zov*' in line 21; an ellipsis at the end of the poem. In line 22 of the version in *Chorb*, the word '*vstanet*' ('stands to') appears, which was changed to '*vsprianet*' ('jumps to/heeds') in *PP*.

I Like That Mountain [*Liubliu ia goru*]
(p. 75)

Dated 31 August 1925, Feldberg (Black Forest) (*PP*). First published in *Rul'* 1459 (19 September 1925), p. 2, without a title, and with 'Schwarzwald' (Black Forest) appearing after the poem, explicitly locating the place of the poem's composition. In *Stikhi* the poem is titled '*Vershina*' ('The Peak'), a title which, as Malikova has noted, Nabokov gives alongside '*Liubliu ia goru*' in his notes to *PP*. Malikova cites postcards Nabokov sent to his mother and to Véra on 31 August; the version sent to his mother bears no title, that to Véra is titled '*Vershina*'. On the postcard to Véra, Nabokov wrote (in Malikova's transcription): 'Shura [Alexandr Zak, a pupil of Nabokov's – Malikova] suggests that I name this poem: What I thought, walking on 31–VIII–25 in Schwarzwald and encountering a familiar plant . . .', and on the same card: 'Transcribe this poem <u>precisely</u> and send it to "*Rul'*" with the request ("My husband . . .") to print it.'

The Dream [*Snovidenie*]
(p. 76)

Dated 22 April 1927 (manuscript); 1927, Berlin (*PP*). First published in *Rul'* 1951 (1 May 1927), p. 2. In the manuscript and the original *Rul'* text, line 4 reads '*i oblegchenno v son vnikaiu*' ('and plunge into sleep with relief'), as opposed to the revised version published in *PP*, '*i oblegchenno v son vstupaiu*' ('and step into sleep with relief'). In the manuscript, an ellipsis follows '*slyshui*' in line 21; and there is an exclamation mark at the end of line 34.

The Snapshot [*Snimok*]
(p. 78)

Dated 20 August 1927, Binz (northern Germany) (*PP*). First published in *Rul'* 2051 (28 August 1927), p. 2; republished in *The Return of Chorb* (1929). In *Chorb* there is a comma after '*pliazhe*' in line 1; a comma after '*morskom*' in line 2; a comma and a dash after '*skat*' in line 18; and a comma after '*dome*' in line 21.

In Paradise [*V raiu*]
(p. 80)

Dated 25 September 1927, Berlin (*PP*). First published in *Rul'* 2223 (18 March 1928), p. 2, under the title '*K dushe*' ('To the soul'). Republished in *The Return of Chorb* (1929) and in *Stikhi* (1979). In *Chorb* there is a comma and a dash after '*dusha*' in line 1; a comma and a dash after '*dikii*' in line 5; an ellipsis after '*sushchestvo*' in line 6; an

ellipsis after '*svoemu*' in line 14; a comma after '*sinem*' in line 15; and
an ellipsis at the end of the poem.

The Execution [*Rasstrel*]
(p. 81)

Dated late 1927, Berlin (*PP*). First published in *Rul'* 2163 (8 January
1928), p. 2. Republished in *The Return of Chorb* (1929). In *Chorb*
there is a comma and a dash after '*liagu*' in line 1; a comma after '*vot*'
in line 3; a comma and a dash after '*prosnus*" in line 5; a comma and
a dash at the end of line 9; a comma after '*vot-vot*' in line 10; a colon
after '*chasov*' in line 14; a comma after '*tak*' in line 18; a dash after
'*rasstrela*' in line 19; and an exclamation mark at the end of the poem.
The following notes are appended to the poem by Nabokov in *PP*:

> Lines 17–20. Freudians have found here a 'death wish,' and Marxists,
> no less grotesquely, 'the expiation of feudal guilt.' I can assure both
> groups that the exclamation in this stanza is wholly rhetorical, a trick
> of style, a deliberately planted surprise, not unlike underpromotion in a
> chess problem.
>
> 'Racemosa' is the name I use for the Russian *cheryomuha*, the 'race-
> mose old-world bird cherry,' *Padus racemosa* Schneider (see my com-
> mentary to *Eugene Onegin*, vol. 3, p. 11).

For Happiness the Lover Cannot Sleep
[*Ot schastiia vliublennomu ne snitsia*]
(p. 82)

Dated 18 May 1928, Berlin (*PP*). The same date is given in the manu-
script. First published in *Rul'* 2293 (14 June 1928), p. 2; republished
as the first poem in *The Return of Chorb* (1929), where it is untitled.
In *Chorb* there is a comma after '*svet*' in line 12 and an ellipsis at
the end of the poem. In the manuscript the poem also ends with an
ellipsis.

Lilith [*Lilit*]
(p. 83)

First published in *PP* (1970), with the following note appended to it
by Nabokov:

Composed more than forty years ago to amuse a friend, 'Lilith' could not be published in any of the sedate *émigré* periodicals of the time. Its manuscript turned up only recently among my old papers. Intelligent readers will abstain from examining this impersonal fantasy for any links with my later fiction.

The Muse [*K muze*]
(p. 85)

Dated 13 September 1929, Berlin (*PP*). First published in *Rul'* 2684 (24 September 1929), p. 2; republished, without a title, in *Stikhotvoreniia* (1952), in which Nabokov states in his author's note that the poem 'marks the end of the period of [his] youthful creativity'. The original *Rul'* version has '*raskryvalsia*' ('disclosed itself') for '*ulybalsia*' ('smiled') in line 8; there is an ellipsis after '*prikhod*' in line 1; and an ellipsis at the end of lines 2, 12, and 23.

Soft Sound [*Tikhii shum*]
(p. 86)

Malikova quotes from a letter about the composition of this poem from Nabokov to Véra of 7 June 1926, which puts it on the previous day. In the notes to *PP*, Nabokov gives the composition as early 1929 in Le Boulou, in southern France, but either his recollection is faulty or (as seems more likely) 1929 is a typo for 1926. First published in *Rul'* 1676 (10 June 1926), p. 4; republished in *The Return of Chorb* (1929). In *Chorb* there is a comma after '*kogda*' in line 1; a comma and a dash after '*otkroesh*'' in line 3, at the end of line 12, after '*shum*' in line 17 and after '*skoroi*' in line 22; a comma at the end of line 21; an ellipsis at the end of line 26 and at the end of the poem; and a dash after '*zato*' in line 29.

Snow [*Sneg*]
(p. 88)

Dated 1930, Berlin (*PP*). First published in *Rul'* 2797 (7 February 1930), p. 2.

The Formula [*Formula*]
(p. 89)

Dated 1931, Berlin (*PP*). First published in *Rul'* 3149 (5 April 1931),
p. 2.

An Unfinished Draft [*Neokonchennyi chernovik*]
(p. 90)

Dated 1931, Berlin (*PP*); 1 July 1931 (Malikova). First published
1970 in *PP*.

Evening on a Vacant Lot [*Vecher na pustyre*]
(p. 91)

Dated 1932, Berlin (*PP*). First published in *Poslednie novosti* (Paris)
4148 (31 July 1932), p. 3, without a title. Republished in *Stikhotvore-
niia* (1952) without the dedication to 'V.D.N.' (his father, Vladimir
Dmitrievich Nabokov).

The Madman [*Bezumets*]
(p. 94)

Dated early 1933, Berlin (*PP*). First published in *Poslednie novosti*
4330 (29 January 1933), p. 3.

How I Love You [*Kak ia liubliu tebia*]
(p. 96)

Dated 17 April 1934, Berlin (Malikova). First published in *Poslednie
novosti* 4788 (3 May 1934), p. 3; republished in *Stikhotvoreniia*
(1952). This translation first appeared in the *New Yorker* 46, no. 44
(23 May 1970), p. 44. In *Zametki*, p. 136, Nabokov comments: '[This
poem], consisting of a few lightly interwoven parts, is addressed at
first as it were to the double of a poet, yearning to return to his home-
land, to some non-existent Russia, out of the foul Germany where
I was then vegetating. The ending is addressed more directly to the
homeland.'

L'Inconnue de la Seine
(p. 98)

The title of the poem in Russian is given in Roman, not Cyrillic, script. First published in *Poslednie novosti* 4844 (28 June 1934), p. 2, without a title but with the subtitle 'From F. G. Ch.' – referring to Fyodor Godunov-Cherdynstev, the protagonist of *The Gift*, which Nabokov was in the early stages of writing at the time. Republished in *Stikhotvoreniia* (1952). 'L'Inconnue de la Seine' was the name given to a mask connected with an unknown young woman drowned in the Seine in the 1860s, which became a popular subject for painters in Paris and Berlin in the 1920s.

At Sunset [*Na zakate*]
(p. 100)

Dated 1935, Berlin (*PP*). First published in *Stikhotvoreniia* (1952). In *Zametki*, p. 135, Nabokov comments on this and similar poems: 'It is perfectly natural that for a young lyricist in exile the loss of his homeland should blend with the loss of love. Out of many such lyric poems of this kind, which I composed in Europe at that time, I have chosen a few, which even now meet my present requirements.'

We So Firmly Believed [*My s toboiu tak verili*]
(p. 101)

Dated 1938, Paris (*PP*). First published 1952 in *Stikhotvoreniia* (1952). Although Nabokov dates this poem to 1938 in *PP*, a manuscript of the poem bears the date January 1939. In several manuscripts, the poem is attributed to Vasilii Shishkov (one of Nabokov's fictional personae), and in one it is dedicated to his close friend Iosif Hessen, as Nabokov acknowledges in *Zametki*, p. 136: '[This] poem is very much fitted to the taste of Iosif Vladimirovich Hessen, a man whose artistic sense and freedom of judgement were so precious to me.'

What Happened Overnight [*Chto za-noch*]
(p. 102)

Dated 1938, Mentone (*PP*). First published in *Stikhotvoreniia* (1952).

The Poets [*Poety*]
(p. 103)

Dated 1939, Paris (*PP*). First published in *Sovremennye zapiski* 69 (July 1939), pp. 262–4, where it is attributed to Vasilii Shishkov (one of Nabokov's fictional personae); republished in *Stikhotvoreniia* (1952), without the attribution to him. In his notes on the poem in *PP*, Nabokov comments:

> The poem was published in a magazine under the pseudonym of 'Vasily Shishkov' in order to catch a distinguished critic (G. Adamovich, of the *Poslednie novosti*) who automatically objected to everything I wrote. The trick worked: in his weekly review he welcomed the appearance of a mysterious new poet with such eloquent enthusiasm that I could not resist keeping up the joke by describing my meetings with the fictitious Shishkov in a story which contained, among other plums, a criticism of the poem and of Adamovich's praise.

> [Lines] 26–27. The streaming emeralds of an aspiring advertisement on the other side of the Seine.

To Russia [*K rossii*]
(p. 105)

Dated late 1939, Paris (*PP*); 16 September 1939, Paris (Malikova). First published in *Sovremennye zapiski* 70 (1940), pp. 128–9, under the title '*Obrashchenie*' ('The Appeal'), and attributed to Vasilii Shishkov (one of Nabokov's fictional personae); republished, without a title, in *Stikhotvoreniia* (1952). In *Zametki*, pp. 136–7, Nabokov states:

> The second poem of this Paris 'cycle' [he is referring to a 'cycle' implicitly begun by 'The Poets'] (as young poets like to put it) was the last of my many addressed to my homeland. It was inspired by a famously filthy pact [the Molotov Pact] between two totalitarian monsters, and if ever after this I addressed myself to Russia, it was only indirectly or through intermediaries.

In a note on the poem in *PP*, he comments on the English translation:

> The original, a streamlined, rapid mechanism, consists of regular three-foot anapests of the 'panting' type, with alternating feminine-masculine

rhymes. It was impossible to combine lilt and literality, except in some passages (only the third stanza gives a close imitation of the poem's form); and since the impetus of the original redeems its verbal vagueness, my faithful but bumpy version is not the success that a prosy cab might have been.

Oculus [*Oko*]
(p. 107)

Dated 1939, Paris (*PP*). First published in *PP* (1970).

Fame [*Slava*]
(p. 108)

Dated 1942, Wellesley, Mass. (*PP*); 22 March 1942, Wellesley, Mass. (Malikova). First published in *Novyi zhurnal* 3 (1942), pp. 157–61; republished in *Stikhotvoreniia* (1952). In *Zametki*, pp. 138, Nabokov comments that

> it is not necessary to say much [about the poem]. I shall say only, that in it a certain devil, resembling a wax figurine, is tempting a free poet with all manner of material rewards. The pseudonym 'Sirin', under which I wrote so much, is referred to in one of the verses in the form of a man, made up as a bird. Those who recall Pushkin's 'Monument' will notice in one place a small paraphrase.

He adds the following notes to the end of the poem in *PP*:

> Line 12/*Akakiy Akakievich*. The hero of Gogol's *Shinel'* (The Carrick) whose speech was interspersed with more or less meaningless accessory words.

> Line 42/*strobe-effect spin*. The term renders exactly what I tried to express by the looser phrase in my text 'sequence of spokelike shadows.' The strobe effect causes wheels to look as if they revolved backward, and the cross over to America (line 36) becomes an optical illusion of a return to Russia.

> Lines 47–48. The injunction is addressed to those – probably nonexisting – readers who might care to decipher an allusion in lines 45–47 to the *sirin*, a fabulous fowl of Slavic mythology, and 'Sirin,' the author's penname in his 1920–1940 period.

Line 67/*gill*. The carton mouthpiece of a Russian cigarette. An unswept floor in a cold room strewn all over with the tubes of discarded cigarette butts used to be a typical platform for the meditations of a hard-up Russian enthusiast in the idealistic past.

Lines 75–76. The references here are to the third stanza of Pushkin's '*Exegi monumentuum*' (1836):

> Tidings of me will cross the whole great Rus,
> and name me will each tribe existing there:
> proud scion of Slavs, and Finn, and the now savage
> Tungus, and – friend of steppes – the Kalmuck

Line 87/*co-orthographical brethren*. A new orthography was introduced in 1917, but *émigré* publications stuck to the old one.

Line 91/*anise-oil*. An allusion to the false fox scent, a drag fooling hounds into following it in lieu of the game.

The Paris Poem [*Parizhskaiia poema*]
(p. 113)

Dated 1943, Cambridge, Mass. (*PP*). First published in *Novyi zhurnal* 7 (1944), pp. 159–63; republished in *Stikhotvoreniia* (1952). In a letter to Wilson of 3 January 1944, Nabokov comments on the composition of this poem that 'I have lain with my Russian muse after a long period of adultery and am sending you the big poem she bore' (*Dear Bunny*, p. 132). He states in *Zametki*, p. 137:

> At its appearance in the New York *Novyi Zhurnal* [this poem] attracted criticism for its murkiness. It becomes clearer, if you keep it in mind that its opening verses represent an attempt of the poet depicted in this poem to conquer the chaotic, inarticulate agitation, when in one's consciousness is dawning only the rhythm of a future creation, but not its direct sense.

Nabokov adds the following notes to the end of the poem in *PP*:

> [Line] 13/*Ot kochúyushchih, prázdno plutáyushchih*. The original imitates much more closely Nekrasov's line calling the poet away 'from those jubilant, those idly babbling' (*ot likuyúshchih, prázdno boltáyushchih*) to the camp (*stan*) of those revolutionaries 'who perish in the name of the great deed of love.' Nikolai Alekseevich Nekrasov

(1821–77), a famous poet who successfully transcended, in a few great poems, the journalist in him, who wrote topical jingles.

[Line] 23/*ostayus's prevideniem*. Lexically: 'I remain with specter,' a play on the closing cliché of *ostayus s uvazheniem*, 'I remain with respect.' Every now and then fidelity receives a miraculous reward.

[Lines] 25–26/*Thus he thought* . . . An allusion to Pushkin's *Eugene Onegin*, first four lines of second stanza:

> Thus a young scapegrace thought,
> with posters flying in the dust,
> by the most lofty will of Zeus
> the heir of all his relatives.

[Line] 64/*Boulevard Arago*. Until quite recently it was there that public decapitations took place in Paris, with local grocers getting the closest view of a reasonably sensational but generally rather messy show.

[Line] 69/*Chuden noch'yu Parizh*. An imitation of a hyperbolic passage in Gogol's *A Terrible Vengeance* (a wretchedly corny tale) which begins: *Chuden Dnepr pri tihoy pogode*, 'wondrous is the Dnepr in windless weather.'

No Matter How [*Kakim by polotnom*]
(p. 118)

Dated 2 April 1943, Cambridge, Mass. (Malikova). First published, without a title, in *Sotsialisticheskii vestnik* (*Socialist Herald*) (New York) 5/6 (17 March 1944); republished in *Stikhotvoreniia* (1952), also without a title. The title was added in *PP*. In *Zametki*, p. 138, Nabokov comments on what inspired the poem:

As is well known, by some strange association of unrelated thoughts, the military glory of Russia has in some haut-bourgeois circles served as a rationale for their acquiescence to the regime. One literary journal, which specialised in this patriotic blather, came to me with a request that I collaborate, and received from me the following, perfectly unexpected, squib.

In a letter to Wilson of 26 March 1944 (*Dear Bunny*, pp. 142–3), Nabokov wrote how

My little impromptu Russian poem about '*Sovetskaia susal'neishaia Rus'*' ['most tinselled Soviet Russia'] has kept 'secretly' circulating in copied and recopied MSS among Russian Socialists of the Kerensky *entourage* affording them the exquisite long-lost thrill of spreading '*zapreshchennye stikhi*' ['forbidden verse'], as they did under the Czars, – until finally one of these Socialists published it anonymously in the *Sotsial[isticheskii] Vestnik* [*Socialist Herald*], introducing it (at the end of an anti-Stalin article) with the special ritualistic cautious manner of reference which was used in the case of MS revolutionary poems half a century ago. The two beautiful points are: 1) such noble civic poems are public property and 2) the poet's name is not divulged because otherwise he would be exiled to Siberia (or Labrador) – by president Roosevelt. If you are familiar with the habitus, *milieu* and style of the Russian left-wing publicist 1845–1945 you will appreciate the delicate fun of the thing.

On Rulers [*O praviteliakh*]
(p. 119)

Dated 1944, Cambridge, Mass. (*PP*). First published in *Novyi zhurnal* 10 (1945), pp. 172–3; republished in *Stikhotvoreniia* (1952). In *Zametki*, p. 137, Nabokov comments how

> [This poem is one of those from the end of the war written] in the sincere civic style. [In it] is intended a parody of the manner of the late Vladimir Mayakovski [see the note on line 52 below]. The rhymes invoked at the end hint at the names of Stalin and (in the Russian pronunciation) Churchill. In this poem is clearly expressed the irritation aroused by those who bow down before thunderers.

In a letter to Nabokov of 17 November 1945, Wilson refers to this poem simply as 'the Mayakovsky parody' (*Dear Bunny*, p. 176). In *PP*, Nabokov includes the following notes on the poem:

> Lines 14–15. Tourists attending performances at Soviet theaters used to be deeply impressed by the late dictator's presence.

> Line 29/*Mamay*. A particularly evil Tartar prince of the fourteenth century.

> Line 35. One recalls Stalin's hilarious pronouncement: 'Life has grown better, life has grown merrier!'

> Lines 42–43. A humorous description of the generously stuffed behind of a Russian coachman in old Russia.

Lines 44–48. A Soviet general and Adolf Hitler make a brief appearance.

Lines 49–50. Our last stop is at Teheran.

Line 52/*my late namesake*. An allusion to the Christian name and patronymic of Vladimir Vladimirovich Mayakovski (1893–1930), minor Soviet poet, endowed with a certain brilliance and bite, but fatally corrupted by the regime he faithfully served.

Lines 58–59/'praline' ... 'air chill.' In the original, *monumentalen*, meaning '[he is] monumental' rhymes pretty closely with *Stalin*; and *pereperchil*, meaning '[he] put in too much pepper,' offers an ingenuous correspondence with the name of the British politician in a slovenly Russian pronunciation ('chair-chill').

To Prince S. M. Kachurin [*K Kn. S. M. Kachurinu*]
(p. 121)

Dated early 1947 (*PP*); March 1947 (Malikova). First published in *Novyi zhurnal* 15 (1947), pp. 81–3; republished in *Stikhotvoreniia* (1952). In *Zametki*, pp. 137–8, Nabokov states how the poem

> is dedicated to my great friend, the famous motor-racer Prince Sergei Mikhailovich Kachurin. Thirty four years ago there arose an opportunity to visit Russia incognito, and my dearest Sergei Mikhailovich very much urged me to make use of this opportunity. I vividly imagined my journey there and wrote [this] poem.

Simon Karlinsky thinks it likely that this is the poem which Nabokov included in a letter to Wilson of 22 February 1947 (*Dear Bunny*, p. 214.) In *PP*, Nabokov includes the following notes on the poem:

> Line 1/*Kachurin*, Stephan Mstislavovich. Pronounced 'Kachoorin' with the accent on the middle syllable. My poor friend, a former White Army colonel, died a few years ago in an Alaskan monastery. The prince's golden heart, moderate brain power, and senile optimism, could alone have been responsible for his suggesting the journey depicted here. His daughter is married to the composer Tornitsen.

> Line 7/*Daghestan*. Alludes to Lermontov's famous poem beginning: 'At noontime, in a dale of Daghestan.'

A Day Like Any Other [*Byl den' kak den'*]
(p. 125)

Dated 1951, Ithaca, NY (*PP*). First published in *Stikhotvoreniia* (1952).

Irregular Iambics [*Nepravil'nye iamby*]
(p. 126)

Dated 5 October 1952, Ithaca, NY (Malikova). First published in *Opyty* (New York) 1 (1953), p. 41, without any division into stanzas and with a misprint. In *PP*, Nabokov includes the following note on the poem's title:

> 'Irregular' (or 'faulty,' *nepravil'nïe*) refers to the fact that in Russian prosody *ésli* (if) is never scudded, as for example the word *mézhdu* (between) is allowed to be by an old tradition. There is no reason, however, why this other light and fluid disyllable should not be treated similarly, especially at the beginning of an iambic line.

What Is the Evil Deed [*Kakoe sdelal ia durnoe delo*]
(p. 127)

Dated 27 December 1959, San Remo (Italy) (*PP*); February 1959 (Malikova, on the basis of a manuscript in the Berg Collection). First published, without a title, in *Vozdushnye puti* (*Aerial Ways*) (New York) 2 (1961), p. 185, as the second poem of a two-part suite entitled 'Two Poems'. In *PP*, Nabokov includes the following note on the poem:

> Lines 1–4. The first strophe imitates the beginning of Boris Pasternak's poem in which he points out that his notorious novel 'made the whole world shed tears over the beauty of [his] native land.'

From the Gray North [*S serogo severa*]
(p. 128)

Dated 20 December 1967, Montreux (*PP*). First published in *Novoe russkoe slovo* (*New Russian Word*) (New York) 20040 (21 January 1968), p. 8, as a holograph photo.

The English Poems from *Poems and Problems*

A Literary Dinner
(p. 131)

First published in the *New Yorker* 18, no. 8 (11 April 1942), p. 18, where it was entitled 'Literary Dinner'.

The Refrigerator Awakes
(p. 132)

First published in the *New Yorker* 18, no. 16 (6 June 1942), p. 20. In a letter to Wilson of 28 November 1941, Nabokov mentions this poem, saying: 'I do hope you did not take my "Refrigerator" as implying that I spent a bad night at your house' (*Dear Bunny*, p. 59).

A Discovery
(p. 134)

Dated no later than 12 January 1943 (Malikova, on the basis of a letter to Edmund Wilson – see *Dear Bunny*, p. 103). First published in the *New Yorker* 19, no. 13 (15 May 1943), p. 26, under the title 'On Discovering a Butterfly' and with 'checkered fringe' for 'checquered fringe' in the version printed in *PP*.

The Poem
(p. 136)

First published in the *New Yorker* 20, no. 17 (10 June 1944), p. 30, with 'eyespotted' for 'eye-spotted' in the version printed in *PP*.

An Evening of Russian Poetry
(p. 137)

First published in the *New Yorker* 21, no. 19 (3 March 1945), pp. 23–4, with '*knowledge crisply browned*' for '*knowledge nicely browned*' in line 18; 'a species of Lucinia comes first' for 'that bird of bards, regale of night, comes first' in line 66; and a comma before 'in conclusion' in line 117. Crucially, the *New Yorker* version does not have the final two lines translating the final two lines in Russian (as Malikova observes). Nabokov sent an early version of this poem to Wilson in a letter of 2 December 1944 (*Dear Bunny*, p. 161).

The Room
(p. 142)

First published in the *New Yorker* 26, no. 17 (13 May 1950), p. 34, with 'shop sign' for 'shopsign' in line 8, and 'afterward' for 'afterwards' in line 17.

Voluptates Tactionum
(p. 144)

First published in the *New Yorker* 26, no. 49 (27 January 1951), p. 30, in a substantially different format to that printed in *PP*:

> Some inevitable day
> On the editorial page of your paper
> It will say, 'Tactio has come of age.'
>
> When you turn a knob,
> Your set will obligingly exhale forms,
> Invisible and yet tangible –
> A world in Braille.
>
> Think of all the things
> That will really be within your reach!
> Phantom bottle,
> Dummy pill,
> Limpid limbs upon a beach.
>
> Grouped before a Magnotact,
> Clubs and families
> Will clutch everywhere
> The same compact paradise
> (In terms of touch).

Palpitating fingertips
Will caress the flossy hair
And investigate the lips
Simulated in mid-air.

See the schoolboy, like a blind lover,
Frantically grope for the shape of love –
And find nothing but the shape of soap.

An early version of this poem was included in a letter sent to Wilson
and his wife on 29 December 1950 (*Dear Bunny*, p. 283).

Restoration
(p. 145)

In *PP*, Nabokov says that this poem was first published in the *New
Yorker*, 9 March 1952, but the *New Yorker* was not published on that
date and I have been unable to locate this poem in any issue of that
magazine. Malikova cites, from the manuscript in the Berg Collec-
tion, two stanzas which were missed out in the printed version of the
poem, one before the initial stanza:

I envy authors who discern
the phoenix in the empty urn,
who find in magic lore a crumb
of comfort – prophecies of some
eternity, of some return

and one before the second stanza:

Before the feast, behind the scenes
I will the world to come apart.
Upon my arm a statue leans,
demands to know what meaning means
and suddenly, with beating heart

with the next stanza beginning: 'Or will there be no great surprise'.

The Poplar
(p. 147)

In *PP*, Nabokov says that this poem was first published in the *New Yorker*, 6 April 1952, but the *New Yorker* wasn't published on that date and I have been unable to locate this poem in any issue of that magazine. Nabokov enclosed this poem in a letter to Wilson of 20 June 1953 (*Dear Bunny*, p. 313).

Lines Written in Oregon
(p. 149)

First published in the *New Yorker* 29, no. 28 (29 August 1953), p. 28. There are three variants: 'Tortured, strangled.) But instead –' for 'Tortured, strangled); but instead –' in line 9; 'road signs' for 'roadsigns' in line 13; and a full stop in place of the semi-colon at the end of line 27. Nabokov enclosed this poem in a letter to Wilson of 20 June 1953 (*Dear Bunny*, p. 313).

Ode to a Model
(p. 151)

First published in the *New Yorker* 31, no. 34 (8 October 1955), p. 48, with a number of variants on the final text as published in *Poems and Problems*. In line 8, after 'stylish', there is a colon rather than a full stop; line 9 begins 'In knee socks and tartan,'; lines 11–12 read 'parted feet pointing outward – / pedal form of akimbo;' and line 13 begins in lower case; line 14 reads 'of Spring and its flowering cherry tree;'; line 16 ends with a semi-colon rather than a full stop; in line 17 'ballerina' is in lower case; lines 19–20 read ' "Can one," somebody asked, / "rhyme 'star' and 'disaster'?" '; line 25 ends with a question mark rather than a dash, and line 26 begins with 'kill' in lower case. In all cases but one, the version in *Poems and Problems* follows that in the 1959 *Poems*. The one exception is that in the 1959 poems, line 14 begins in lower case, as in the *New Yorker*, though already the word 'flowering' has been removed.

On Translating 'Eugene Onegin'
(p. 153)

First published in the *New Yorker* 30, no. 47 (8 January 1955), p. 34, with a variant in the final line – 'The shadow of your monument' – and with the subheading 'An Illustration of the "Onegin" Stanza – Metre and Rhyme Pattern'. Nabokov placed this poem after 'Ode to a Model' in *PP*, even though this is contrary to the chronological sequence he otherwise observed in ordering the poems in that volume.

Rain
(p. 154)

First published in the *New Yorker* 32, no. 9 (21 April 1956), p. 43, with three variants: line 8 begins in lower case; line 9 ends with a semi-colon; and there is no comma after 'past' at the end of line 11.

The Ballad of Longwood Glen
(p. 155)

This poem was first offered to the *New Yorker* in 1953 (Malikova). First published in the *New Yorker* 33, no. 20 (6 July 1957), p. 27, with two minor variants. Instead of 'Every paper had: Man Lost in Tree.', the original has 'Every paper had "MAN LOST IN TREE."' and 'Rest rooms' rather than 'Restrooms' in line 58. Nabokov comments on the poem in a number of letters. Writing to Wilson on 15 October 1953, he refers to it as 'a ballad I wrote some time ago' (*Dear Bunny*, p. 314). In a letter of 16 February 1957 to Katharine White at the *New Yorker*, he writes: 'I am sending you a little ballad you turned down in 1953. I still think it is one of the best things I ever wrote. On second thought – tell me first if I may send it again' (*Selected Letters*, p. 201). In a letter to White of 6 March of the same year (*Selected Letters*, pp. 208–9), he says:

> I am sending you *The Ballad of Longwood Glen*, which I wrote in 1953. Ever since then I have been reworking it, so that this final product differs considerably from the one which The New Yorker rejected some three years ago. I want to ask you to consider it very carefully. With my

usual modesty I maintain it is the best poem I have composed – far superior, for instance, to the *Evening of Russian Poetry.*

At first blush the ballad may look to you like a weird hybrid between Shagall and Grandmother Moses. But please stick to it as long as you can bear, and by degrees all kinds of interesting shades and underwater patterns will be revealed to the persevering eye. If you still hate it, please feel no qualms – just send it back.

English Poems Not Included in *Poems and Problems*

Home
(p. 161)

First published in the *Trinity Magazine* (Cambridge) 2, no. 5 (November 1920), p. 26. Signed 'Vladimir Nabokoff'.

Remembrance
(p. 162)

First published in the *English Review* (London) 144 (November 1920), p. 392. Signed 'Vladimir Nabokoff'.

The Russian Song
(p. 163)

Dated 17 February 1923 (manuscript). First published in *Carrousel* (Berlin) 2 (1923).

Softest of Tongues
(p. 164)

Dated 21 October 1941, Wellesley, Mass. (manuscript). First published in the *Atlantic Monthly* 168, no. 6 (December 1941), p. 765. In the typescript it is entitled 'Farewell Party'.

Exile
(p. 165)

Dated 13 September 1942 (Malikova). First published in the *New Yorker* 18, no. 36 (24 October 1942), p. 26. Wilson thought this the best of Nabokov's English poems. In a letter to him of 13 September 1942, Nabokov comments that, having composed a poem in fourth paeons within ten minutes, the 'composing of the amphibrachic poem ['Exile'] proved more difficult. I had to struggle against slipping into anapest, just as there are horses that *sbivaiutsia s ryssi na galop* [break from a trot into a gallop]. I have tried to relieve the jogging monotony of the meter by using various enjambements and shortening every third line' (*Dear Bunny*, p. 92).

A Poem
(p. 166)

Dated 11 November 1942, Saint Paul, Minn. (Malikova). First published in the *Atlantic Monthly* 171, no. 1 (January 1943), p. 116. Malikova notes that in the typescript in the Berg Collection this poem is entitled 'A War Poem'.

Dream
(p. 167)

Dated 16 August 1944, Cambridge, Mass. (Malikova). First published in the *Atlantic Monthly* 178, no. 3 (September 1946), p. 63. Nabokov sent this poem to Wilson in a letter to him of 16 August 1944. In another letter, 2 March 1946, he refers to it as 'the nightmare poem returned last year by the *N[ew] Y[orker]* ...' (*Dear Bunny*, pp. 155, 187).

Dandelions
(p. 168)

Dated 30 May 1950, Ithaca, NY (manuscript). First published in *Russian Literature Triquarterly* 24 (1991), in which the manuscript of the poem is reproduced.

Lunar Lines
(p. 169)

First published in the *New York Review of Books* 6, no. 7 (28 April 1966), p. 19. The poem was probably inspired by the first unmanned moon landing (by the Russians).

Index of Titles

Index of First Lines

First-time Publication Details

Please note that previous versions of some of the poems contain occasional variants, which are recorded in the endnotes for this new Penguin edition. First publication of the original Russian text for each poem is given in that section too.

Poems by Vladimir Nabokov

Translations of Russian poems from *Poems and Problems*: all the translations first appeared in that volume (New York: McGraw-Hill, 1970), with the exception of 'How I Love You', which first appeared in the *New Yorker* 46, no. 44 (23 May 1970), p. 44.

English poems from *Poems and Problems*: these were all previously published elsewhere, aside from 'The Poplar' and 'Restoration'. (In his notes to *Poems and Problems*, Nabokov says that these poems were published in the *New Yorker*; I have found no record of them either in the edition he specifies or in the rest of the New Yorker archive.)

'The Ballad of Longwood Glen', *New Yorker* 33, no. 20 (6 July 1957), p. 27

'A Discovery', *New Yorker* 19, no. 13 (15 May 1943), p. 26 (entitled 'On Discovering a Butterfly')

'An Evening of Russian Poetry', *New Yorker* 21, no. 19 (3 March 1945), pp. 23–4

'Lines Written in Oregon', *New Yorker* 29, no. 28 (29 August 1953), p. 28

'A Literary Dinner', *New Yorker* 18, no. 8 (11 April 1942), p. 18 (entitled 'Literary Dinner')

'Ode to a Model', *New Yorker* 31, no. 34 (8 October 1955), p. 48

'On Translating "Eugene Onegin"', *New Yorker* 30, no. 47 (8 January 1955), p. 34

'The Poem', *New Yorker* 20, no. 17 (10 June 1944), p. 30
'Rain', *New Yorker* 32, no. 9 (21 April 1956), p. 43
'The Refrigerator Awakes', *New Yorker* 18, no. 16 (6 June 1942),
    p. 20
'The Room', *New Yorker* 26, no. 17 (13 May 1950), p. 34
'Voluptates Tactionum', *New Yorker* 26, no. 49 (27 January 1951),
    p. 30

English poems not included in *Poems and Problems*:

'Dandelions', *Russian Literature Triquarterly* 24 (1991)
'Dream', *Atlantic Monthly* 178, no. 3 (September 1946), p. 63
'Exile', *New Yorker* 18, no. 36 (24 October 1942), p. 26
'Home', *Trinity Magazine* (Cambridge) 2, no. 5 (November 1920),
    p. 26
'Lunar Lines', *New York Review of Books* 6, no. 7 (28 April 1966),
    p. 19
'A Poem', *Atlantic Monthly* 171, no. 1 (January 1943), p. 116
'Remembrance', *English Review* (London) 144 (November 1920),
    p. 392
'The Russian Song', *Carrousel* (Berlin) 2 (1923)
'Softest of Tongues', *Atlantic Monthly* 168, no. 6 (December 1941),
    p. 765

Poems translated by Dmitri Nabokov

Translations published for the first time in this edition:

'Cubes'
'The Hawkmoth'
'Music'
'A Trifle'
'The University Poem'

Translations previously published elsewhere:

'Butterflies', *Nabokov's Butterflies*, edited by Brian Boyd and Rob-
    ert Michael Pyle (Boston: Beacon Press, 2000), p. 121
'The Demon', Nabokovian 28 (Spring 1992), pp. 34–5
'Dream', *Areté* 13 (Winter 2003), p. 9
'Easter', *Areté* 13 (Winter 2003), pp. 12–13

'Evening', *Areté* 13 (Winter 2003), pp. 16–17 (an earlier version of the translation was published in *The Achievements of Vladimir Nabokov*, edited by G. Gibian and S. J. Parker (Ithaca, NY: Cornell University Press, 1984), pp. 168–9)

'Fortune-telling', *Nabokovian* 43 (Fall 1999), p. 44

'Forty-three years, forty-four years maybe', *Nabokovian* 40 (Spring 1998), pp. 12–13

'The Glasses of St Joseph', *Nabokovian* 54 (Spring 2005), p. 4

'I have no need, for my nocturnal travels', *Nabokovian* 40 (Spring 1998), pp. 8–11

'The Last Supper', *Nabokovian* 60 (Spring 2008), pp. 6–7

'Like pallid dawn, my poetry sounds gently', *Nabokovian* 43 (Fall 1999), pp. 16–17

'Peter in Holland', *Nabokovian* 51 (Fall 2003), p. 4

'Revolution', *Paris Review* 175 (Fall/Winter 2005), pp. 171–3

'The Ruler', *Nabokovian* 24 (Spring 1990), pp. 46–9

'St Petersburg', *Nabokovian* 42 (Spring 1999), pp. 6–8

'Shakespeare', the *Nabokovian* 20 (Spring 1988), pp. 15–16

'The Skater', *Areté* 13 (Winter 2003), pp. 16–17

'Spring', *Nabokovian* 28 (Spring 1992), pp. 36–9

'Tolstoy', *New York Review of Books* 35, no. 3 (3 March 1988), p. 6

'To the Grapefruit', the *Nabokovian* 42 (Spring 1999), pp. 38–9

'To Véra', *Nabokovian* 23 (Fall 1989), pp. 13–4

'The Train Wreck', *Nabokovian* 22 (Spring 1989), pp. 12–17

'Ut Pictura Poesis', *Nabokovian* 51 (Fall 2003), pp. 28–31 (republished in *Areté* 13 (Winter 2003), pp. 14–15)

Nabokov on first love

Mary

In a Berlin boarding house filled with an assortment of curious Russian émigrés, Lev Ganin, a young officer poised between his past and his future, relives his first love affair. His memories of Mary are suffused with the freshness of youth and the idyllic ambience of pre-revolutionary Russia. *Mary*, Nabokov's first novel, is a gripping evocation of the pangs of young love and the power of memory.

The Gift

Fyodor is an aspiring young writer living in 1920s Berlin, who dreams of the great book he will someday write. This is the story of Fyodor's all-engulfing passion for writing, his attempts to be a success, his yearning for his native land and his relationship with the elusive Zina; a tale of remembrance, secrets, family, time, art, lost keys and butterfly-catchers that is infused with love.

The Enchanter

A middle-aged, well-off, outwardly respectable man sits on a park bench, contemplating the depths of his 'murky soul'. When he spies a coltish, russet-haired beauty on roller skates, he makes it his mission to seduce her, even if he must marry her ailing mother to do so. Anticipating Nabokov's masterpiece *Lolita*, this playful, mischievous and perfectly crafted story is at once hilarious and chilling.

Nabokov on nostalgia

Speak, Memory

'Speak, memory' said Vladimir Nabokov. And immediately a host of enchanting recollections came flooding back to him in this rich, captivating autobiography: of his comfortable childhood and adolescence, of his rich, liberal-minded father, his beautiful mother and of grand old houses in St Petersburg and the surrounding countryside in pre-revolutionary Russia.

The Luzhin Defense

Discovering his prodigious gift in boyhood, rising to the rank of international Grandmaster, chess-playing genius Luzhin develops a lyrical passion for the game that renders the real world a phantom. Playful, ingenious and endearing, *The Luzhin Defense* intimately conveys the sensations of a child's world.

Glory

Martin Edelweiss is a romantic and aimless young Russian who has fled his homeland after the revolution. When his mother sends him to study in England, where he is taken in by a family of fellow Russian émigrés, Martin becomes dominated by his passion for their daughter Sonia. Told through dreamlike vignettes, *Glory* is an exquisite depiction of memory and the imagination.

Nabokov's great satirical works

Lolita

Humbert Humbert – scholar, aesthete and romantic – has fallen completely and utterly in love with Lolita Haze, his landlady's gum-snapping, silky skinned twelve-year-old daughter. Reluctantly agreeing to marry Mrs Haze just to be close to Lolita, Humbert suffers greatly in the pursuit of romance; but when Lo herself starts looking for attention elsewhere, he will carry her off on a desperate cross-country misadventure, all in the name of Love. Hilarious, flamboyant, heart-breaking and full of ingenious wordplay, *Lolita* is an immaculate, unforgettable masterpiece of obsession, delusion and lust.

'Lolita is comedy, subversive yet divine' Martin Amis

Pnin

Professor Timofey Pnin, previously of Tsarist Russia, is now precari-ously positioned at the heart of an American campus. Battling comi-cally with American life and language, Pnin must face great hazards in this new world: the ruination of his beautiful lumber-room-as-office; the removal of his teeth and the fitting of new ones; the search for a suitable boarding-house; and the trials of taking the wrong train. Hilarious, intelligent and moving, *Pnin* reveals the absurd side of a national exile.

'Nabokov can move you to laughter in the way that masters can – to laughter that is near to tears' *Guardian*

Nabokov's great satirical works

Despair

Self-satisfied, delighting in the many fascinating quirks of his own personality, Hermann Hermann is perhaps not to be taken too seriously. But then a chance meeting with Felix, a man he believes to be his double, reveals a frightening 'split' in Hermann's nature. Filled with impudent, startling humour, *Despair* takes us into a deranged world of doubles and illusions.

Invitation to a Beheading

Sentenced to death, exploring his prison cell as he counts down his final days, Cincinnatus cannot find out when his execution will occur and is troubled by the lack of control he has over his own life. Witty and nightmarish, *Invitation to a Beheading* creates a dystopian and fantastical world, exploring the unusual hope a man may carry to his death.

Bend Sinister

The state has recently been taken over by the tyrannical and philistine 'Average Man' party. Only Adam Krug, a brilliant philosopher, stands up to the regime, seeing no threat to his loved ones, but the party set in motion sinister machinations. Nabokov's dark fable is a nuanced portrayal of totalitarianism and 'dim-brained brutality', but also of Krug's enduring love for his family.

www.penguinclassics.com

*Contemporary ... Provocative ... Outrageous ...
Prophetic ... Groundbreaking ... Funny ... Disturbing ...
Different ... Moving ... Revolutionary ... Inspiring ...
Subversive ... Life-changing ...*

What makes a modern classic?

At Penguin Classics our mission has always been to make the best
books ever written available to everyone. And that also means
constantly redefining and refreshing exactly what makes a 'classic'.
That's where Modern Classics come in. Since 1961 they have been an
organic, ever-growing and ever-evolving list of books from the last
hundred (or so) years that we believe will continue to be read over and
over again.

They could be books that have inspired political dissent, such as
Animal Farm. Some, like *Lolita* or *A Clockwork Orange*, may have
caused shock and outrage. Many have led to great films, from *In Cold
Blood* to *One Flew Over the Cuckoo's Nest*. They have broken down
barriers – whether social, sexual, or, in the case of *Ulysses*, the
boundaries of language itself. And they might – like *Goldfinger* or
Scoop – just be pure classic escapism. Whatever the reason, Penguin
Modern Classics continue to inspire, entertain and enlighten millions
of readers everywhere.

'No publisher has had more influence on reading habits than Penguin'
Independent

'Penguins provided a crash course in world literature'
Guardian

The best books ever written

PENGUIN (◊) CLASSICS

SINCE 1946

Find out more at www.penguinclassics.com